A Will To Believe

Oxford Wells Shakespeare Lectures

Believe

Shakespeare and Religion

DAVID SCOTT KASTAN

OXFORD
UNIVERSITY PRESS

OXFORD
UNIVERSITY PRESS

Great Clarendon Street, Oxford, OX2 6DP,
United Kingdom

Oxford University Press is a department of the University of Oxford.
It furthers the University's objective of excellence in research, scholarship,
and education by publishing worldwide. Oxford is a registered trade mark of
Oxford University Press in the UK and in certain other countries

First Edition published in 2014

Impression: 2

Published in the United States of America by Oxford University Press
198 Madison Avenue, New York, NY 10016, United States of America

British Library Cataloguing in Publication Data

Data available

Library of Congress Control Number: 2013942194

ISBN 978–0–19–957289–2

Printed in Great Britain by
Clays Ltd, St Ives plc

For Jane, forever

Acknowledgments

This book began as a series of lectures I was privileged to give at Oxford in the autumn of 2008. Sponsored by the Faculty of English and Oxford University Press, the occasion was then a new event on the University calendar: the Oxford Wells Shakespeare Lectures, designed to honor Stanley Wells and his remarkable career as a critic and an editor of Shakespeare. I was enormously flattered to be invited to inaugurate this series, although I remain worried that neither in performance nor in print are they worthy of the scholarly career they were meant to celebrate. By almost any possible measure, Stanley is the most significant Shakespeare scholar of his generation, and his work, both critical and editorial, will continue to shape Shakespeare studies for other scholars as well as for students and general readers. Arguably he is Shakespeare's most important modern collaborator. It was, therefore, nerve-wracking to deliver these with Stanley sitting in the front row, though he would graciously smile when I caught his eye, a response, which, had he withheld it, I fear might have left me unable to continue. So it is first of all his generosity that I must acknowledge and thank.

Others, of course, must be thanked as well, although also with my full recognition of the meagerness of this expression of gratitude in relation to the magnitude of the kindness that was on offer. The Faculty of English, the University Press, St Catherine's College, Merton College, and Wolfson College (which put on a perfect "American" Thanksgiving dinner on the proper day after the final lecture) were spectacular hosts, introducing me to (and spoiling me with) the many social and intellectual delights of Oxford, which previously I had known of only from my reading of academic novels. I do want to thank by name Hermione Lee, Richard McCabe, Andrew McNellie, and Bart van Es, who could not have been more gracious, genial, and helpful, but also everyone at the University and the Press who worked to make this occasion both possible and memorable. And it should be noted that it only rained once in the fortnight in which I was a guest at Oxford, though I am reluctant to give credit for that to any of those mentioned, even to Stanley. I should say that the chapters published here are somewhat revised from the form in which they were delivered at Oxford. I hope that what they have gained both in clarity and from the opportunity to take into account at least some of the wonderful work that has been done in this field since they were first written is more than fair compensation for the loss of whatever liveliness marked the occasions of the original lectures. I will admit to being unable to give up some of what seemed, at least to me, to be funny when they were delivered. I hope that bit of self-indulgence seems worthwhile to readers.

There are other people whose contributions must be recognized, but whose effect on what is here is impossible to acknowledge adequately: the great number of scholars whose work on the topics touched on in this book has been instrumental in inspiring and shaping my own thinking about them. Some of these are scholars known to me only in print, and whose work I hope is appropriately recognized in my endnotes and with my efforts to engage with it. And there are others with whom I have also been privileged to have had ongoing conversations about these issues, in some cases lasting over decades, some of whom have graciously read and commented on (and then still reread) versions of the chapters of this book. It would have been impossible to write it without the contributions of Euan Cameron, John Cox, Brian Cummings, Margreta de Grazia, Lori Anne Ferrell, Tom Freeman, Bruce Gordon, Stephen Greenblatt, Brad Holden, Jesse Lander, Peter Lake, Leah Marcus, Rich McCoy, Claire McEachern, Larry Manley, Arthur Marotti, Robert Miola, Glynn Parry, Annabel Patterson, Kristen Poole, Aaron Pratt, Regina Schwartz, Debora Shuger, Jim Shapiro, Alison Shell, Peter Stallybrass, Daniel Swift, Dan Vitkus, Michael Warner, and Keith Wrightson.

A long list for a short book, and yet I know the list should be still longer and my gratitude more effusive. If ever good deeds were "shuffled off with such uncurrent pay," it is here. Let this stand as my thanks, my apology, and an IOU for a drink to those who know themselves shortchanged. Most of the ones named have already had that drink, some several times over, but there will be still more to come. Bruce Gordon, Brad Holden, and Claire McEachern also get a dinner.

But most importantly and completely insufficiently, once again I say thank you for so much more than can ever be specified to the person to whom this book is dedicated—and with my promise that I will at long last clear off the dining room table.

Contents

1

Introduction: A Will to Believe

He puns tortuously and despairingly on the many
possible senses of the word "will."

Stanley Wells

When I first began working on the lecture series upon which this
book is based, I planned to call it *Will and Grace*, momentarily thinking that it would make a terrifically witty title for a consideration of
Shakespeare and early modern religion. But of course not the least
of the dangers of pop culture references is that they date themselves
too quickly. The TV sitcom from which I planned to borrow my
title would soon go off the air—and even in its heyday was hardly
noticed anywhere other than in America. But the title I settled on,
A Will to Believe, if it successfully avoids the appalling Scylla of faux
hipness, undoubtedly still falls victim to the dismaying Charybdis of
predictability. In truth, the "Will" pun for anything about Shakespeare
was probably already exhausted once Sonnet 135 appeared in print
in 1609. Just in the last few years we have had, among others, *Will
Power*, *Poetic Will*, *Reading Shakespeare's Will*, *Will in the World*, *Contested
Will*, and *Women of Will*.[1]

Nonetheless, I am still holding on to my chosen title for its particular condensation of the set of concerns that interests me. *A Will
to Believe* obviously gestures at Shakespeare himself and the question
of what he might have believed, and glances at his legal will, which
may or may not tell us anything about his own beliefs. And "will,"
of course, is a much discussed theological term—to what degree it
is free, and to what ends it is efficacious—while our "will to believe"
is, in a different sense, a condition of the plays' success on the page
or in the theater.

A Will to Believe also alludes directly to a famous essay by William James.[2] I am not claiming Shakespeare as a proto-Jamesian, but I do want to invoke James's understanding that religion is not a matter of instinct or intuition, but of what he somewhat confusingly calls "will." For James this "will to believe" is not mere volition or even inspiration (God's will). It is some mix of "fear and hope, prejudice and passion, imitation and partisanship, the circumpressure of our cast and set."[3] James's will in this sense crystallizes the combination of the personal and the cultural, the psychological and the theological, the anxiety and the joy that historians have identified in the religious experience of early modern England, and that seems visible in Shakespeare's understanding of religion in the plays.

For James, however, religious experience, which he defines as inward and primary, was always valued more highly than religious life, which is social and, for him, derivative. In some obvious ways, James is in this regard merely the heir of the Reformation, although he fails to recognize how the very inwardness that for him is fundamental to his idea of religion had been authorized and transmitted by a religious collectivity he cannot fully credit. But he recognizes that one can have and demonstrate a "will to believe," while understanding that faith is always the gift of grace.[4]

For Shakespeare, the collectivity seemingly mattered more than it did for James, maybe mattered even more than did the inwardness, if only because it was so very inward: "Then is there mirth in heaven,/When earthly things made even/Atone together" (*As You Like It*, 5.4.106–8). But in post-Reformation England atoning together could often be easier to imagine than to achieve. Jesus would prophesy: "Think ye that I haue come to giue peace on earth? I tell you, nay, but rather debate" (Luke 12:51). Certainly early modern England would hear plenty of debate in Christ's name.

This book is, at least in part, about how that debate registers in the plays of Shakespeare. In post-Reformation England, the divisive confessionalism[5] served to highlight religion, making it impossible that it could be an unremarkable given of the culture. I am not claiming Shakespeare as a partisan in those debates. He wasn't one. I am not claiming him even as a believer. I don't know what or even if he believed. But I am claiming what seems undeniable: that he recognized and responded to the various ways in which religion charged the world in which he lived. For some, religion was experienced with certainty and joy, for some with doubt and even despair. Sometimes it bound communities together; sometimes it tore them apart. Most often it was habitual, not therefore unimportant but important precisely for that reason.

On 19 December 1601, John Croke, then Speaker of the House of Commons, addressed his colleagues: "If a question should be asked, What is the first and chief thing in a Commonwealth to be regarded? I should say, religion. If, What is the second? I should say, religion. If, What the third? I should still say, religion." For Croke, religion was "the sure and firm band binding us in devotion and piety to God."[6] But if religion bound the English faithful to God, it didn't always seem to bind the English to one another. Montaigne had called religion, in John Florio's 1603 translation, "the most important subject, that possibly can be," although he noted that in England the official forms of worship had "been changed and rechanged three or foure times."[7] The religious history of England provided him with a particular instance of what seemed a universal truth: "marke if wee doe not handle it [i.e. religion] as it were a peece of waxe, from out of so right and so firme a rule, to draw so many contrary shapes" (sig. Z1^v). Certainly early modern England saw its official religion drawn into "contrary shapes" as its prescribed forms of worship lurched from one to another under different monarchs, but in whatever shapes it was experienced it was there, prominent and persistent.

There was a more or less universal belief in God, though the Reformation had ensured that religion was something experienced in the parochial terms in which that belief found purchase in individual souls. Early modern Christians almost never worried if God existed, but rather about what He expected of them in order to be saved, even though, as Christopher Haigh has recently argued, most people "didn't think God expected very much."[8] But religion also served as the epistemological ground organizing the fundamental categories of thought, so it was no less—and arguably more—important as culture than as belief.[9] Its disputed etymology—from the Latin *relegere*: "to read again," or *religare*: "to bind"—tells its double story.

Yet for all its seemingly inescapable centrality, it still would not
have been that long ago that a book about Shakespeare and religion
would have seemed odd—and probably tendentious—in a way that
one on, say, Spenser and religion or Milton and religion would obviously have not, or possibly even religion and any other early modern writer. And while today a book about Shakespeare and anything
else *but* religion might possibly seem odd, it is still hard to argue that,
whatever the poems and plays might suggest about Shakespeare's
own belief, his writings display the same kind of religious concern or
commitment as Spenser's or Milton's verse.

It isn't merely that he is a playwright and they are poets, though
that is not without consequence for their differentiation. It is mostly
that the plays are not motivated by similar considerations of doctrine or of Church government. They were not written to give form
to a conception of holiness or to promote some polemical position
in the fractious world of post-Reformation England. They were
intended neither as prophecy nor as propaganda. They do not set
out either to celebrate the "discipline of faith and veritie" (*Faerie
Queene*, 1.6.31.9) or to "justify the ways of God to men" (*Paradise
Lost*, 1.26).

Interest in Spenser and Milton has, however, been reanimated (at
least within the academy, sadly the only place where this has happened) precisely by insisting on the intricate relationship between
their poetry and the charged religious environment in which it was
written and read. Their verse both presupposes some truth about
Christianity and can be thought if not actively to promote it, at least
energetically to engage it.

Religion in Shakespeare seems different. It has always seemed
different. Spenser and Milton have been salvaged for modern readers largely by recognizing the ways in which the poetry takes form
and urgency from their religious investments; Shakespeare had,
almost from the beginning, been valued for his apparent freedom
from them. What has been identified as the mark, if not also the
enabling condition, of his capacious imagination is his putative
independence, in Joseph Ritson's phrase, from "the reigning superstition of the time."[10] Shakespeare has been seen to rise above the
confessional commitments and the polemical enthusiasms that
shaped his historical moment to define terms of humanity that have

come to seem more essential than these: his subject is human life in all its particularity.

Shakespeare becomes the creator for whom the term is not a near blasphemy, a god for a culture in which faith has become a more or less voluntary commitment within an expansive field of confessional possibility, and his plays become its scripture. Though Dryden seems to be the first person to call Shakespeare "divine,"[11] by 1728 Voltaire could contemptuously write that "Shakespeare, their leading tragic poet, is rarely called anything *but* 'divine' in England," and by the middle of the century, Arthur Murphy would proudly confirm that Shakespeare was "a kind of established religion." By the end of the nineteenth century, as Henry Morley said, "All who read Shakespeare are content to hear his works described as a Lay Bible."[12] And in our own time, Harold Bloom would echo the exact sentiments in his claim that the plays have "the status of a secular Bible" and his insistence that "Bardolotry, the worship of Shakespeare, ought to be even more a secular religion than it already is."[13]

Such terms of enthusiasm, however, seem misconceived, except as intensive registers of Shakespeare's undoubted cultural importance. The language works only to mystify Shakespeare, if not actually to mislead. It is never quite clear what claim is being made, not only because "secular" has become itself such a contested notion,[14] but also because casting his excellence in religious language has, paradoxically, often allowed us to neglect or misunderstand the religious language and concerns that actually animate the plays.

Shakespeare neither ignores religion nor provides some alternative path to its truths. Santayana notoriously saw him as a playwright for whom it was the "absence of religion" that most obviously defined his writing and was "a sign of his good sense."[15] But that seems no less a misreading than Piero Boitani's recent *Gospel According to Shakespeare*, a book whose "plot" moves "from *Hamlet* to *King Lear*, where Shakespeare's New Testament is only announced and where faith, salvation, and peace are only glimpsed at from far away, and on to *Pericles*, *Cymbeline*, *The Winter's Tale*, and *The Tempest*, where the themes of transcendence, immanence, the role of the deity, resurrection, and epiphany are openly, if often obliquely, staged."[16] Shakespeare is not Dante, but neither is he Dreiser.

Religion is central in the plays, but Shakespeare is not a religious playwright, at least not in the sense that the Wakefield master or John Bale, or even William Wager, might be thought one. Goethe wrote that "the interests which vitalize Shakespeare's great genius are interests which center in this world."[17] This seems to me right, but only with the proviso that "this world," as Shakespeare knows and writes it, is one in which religion is salient. It emerges in the plays as something too fundamental, and sometimes too recalcitrant, to be seen merely as local color or as raw material to be shaped by his artistic will. The plays too clearly assume a world in which God is immanent, even if that immanence is not their subject.

Religion provides Shakespeare with the fundamental language of value and understanding in the plays, from the beginning of his career through its end. It supplies the vocabulary in which characters understand themselves and are presented to us to be understood. Dromio of Ephesus can pun about his ill treatment: "Mistress, *respice finem*; respect your end; or rather, to prophesy like the parrot, beware the rope's end" (*Comedy of Errors*, 4.4.39–41). Romeo says to Juliet, "Call me but love and I'll be new baptized" (2.1.92). Richard II, forced to participate publicly in his deposition, accuses the onlookers: "you Pilates/Have here delivered me to my sour cross/And water cannot wash away your sins" (4.1.240–2). Rosalind praises Orlando's wooing: "his kissing is as full of sanctity as the touch of holy bread" (*As You Like It*, 3.4.12–13). Iago knows that "to the jealous" trivial things can seem "confirmations strong/As proofs of holy writ" (*Othello*, 3.3.326–7), while Emilia can joke that she would "venture purgatory" (4.3.7) to make her husband a monarch. Holding the dagger in his bloodstained hand, Macbeth hears the grooms cry out, but "List'ning their fear, I could not say 'amen'/When they did say 'God bless us'" (2.2.31–2). Prospero is certain that his "ending is despair,/Unless I be relieved by prayer,/Which pierces so that it assaults/Mercy itself and frees all faults" (*The Tempest*, Epi. 15–18).

Measure for Measure is itself a biblical allusion (Mark 4:24 or Matthew 7:2), and scholars have identified hundreds of additional references in the plays, though these resist neat confessional assignment. Even in the classical tragedies the Christian vocabulary appears, as in *Titus Andronicus*, where the evil Aaron, admitting that he does not believe in any god, nonetheless demands an oath from Lucius that he will save Aaron's child: "I know thou art religious/ And hast a thing within thee called conscience"; and this strange notion of "conscience" is immediately coded in conspicuously anachronistic terms: "with twenty popish tricks and ceremonies/Which I have seen thee carefully to observe" (5.1.74–7).

What is everywhere evident is Shakespeare's awareness of the inescapability of religion in his England. He is attentive to the fundamental, if sometimes fiercely debated terms in which people sought to understand their own lives and their relationships to their families, communities, and God; and he is equally mindful of its sheer ordinariness, as, say, with the reflexive "God b'wi' you" in leave taking. Such conventional phrases provide more telling evidence of the embeddedness of religion in the language itself than a confirmation of the speaker's faith, though much more of the residue of their literal meaning survives in these expressions than in the reflexive "God bless you" today in response to a sneeze.

To ignore the ways in which religious language and concerns saturate the plays is obviously to miss something essential about them, though to use them to decide Shakespeare's own religious convictions or sympathies seems to me no less a mistake. We may discover his characteristic habits of mind in his presentation of controversial material, but his own faith cannot be teased out of his handling of the controversies. Shakespeare declines to tell us what to believe, or to tell us what he believed. But this is not the familiar claim of his disinterested secularism, for he shows us that human beings do believe and in their various and variant beliefs, they discover and create complex relations to their pasts and their futures.

It is this experience of belief that engages Shakespeare rather than the truth of what was believed. The plays are neither coded statements about his faith nor are they modes of religious thinking—although they are modes of thinking about religion as it is lived, but that's not quite the same thing. Religion in the plays is a psychological and social reality that registers as form, rather than a credal one that registers as belief. The plays matter not as theology but because they provide a "bristling sensual record of the instance," in the characteristically bristling sensual phrase of my first English professor.[18] Shakespeare creates a series of hypothetical worlds, which look and sound like reality, but, of course, aren't. They respond to it, even participate in it, but their own artistry is the enigmatic excess that differentiates the plays from other discursive forms and marks them, as with all works of art, as something *in themselves* to be noticed. Perhaps that alone insists they are something other than religious, encouraging our participation on a very different set of terms.

But, in whatever ways, we now see religion among the concerns that are legible in the plays. Oddly, the post-theoretical embrace of history in both new historicism and cultural materialism had usually ignored religion or treated it instrumentally as an aspect of governmental control, in which the world was the end and faith merely the means to it. Scholars, however, have now appropriately insisted on returning lived religion to the discussion of Shakespeare's writings. We recognize it now as an essential, if often perplexing dimension of early modern identity, and we sense its haunting presence in Shakespeare's plays, even if we do not know precisely how to account for this and are not sure exactly what it might mean.

Yet even as religion has been returned to our discussions of early modern drama, we often claim either too little or too much for it, especially when we shift from what characters say to what performance does. No longer content to see playing as merely reflective, holding the mirror up to nature, we have come to recognize it as more socially productive, in one influential understanding seeing it as a surrogate for a Church that no longer satisfies the affective needs of many people.[19] The spectacular success of the newly commercialized theater in the last quarter of the sixteenth century is seen to derive from its ability to function as a form of restitution and repair, perhaps in the process even becoming, in a particularly optimistic version of this narrative, "the first truly Reformed church."[20]

I am not sure I understand exactly what "truly" means in this phrase, but I see the point. It is a view of theater as compensation, providing our finest examples, in Salman Rushdie's phrase, of what are "most likely to fill our god-shaped holes."[21] The post-Reformation theater replaces and exploits the emotional spaces left empty by the loss of ritual (although it is less common in many of these accounts to consider carefully to what degree ritual in early modern England was in fact lost).

For all the rich suggestiveness and impressive sophistication of the argument, however, it still doesn't seem quite right to me as an account of what the religious language, values, practices, spaces, and personnel are doing in the plays or of what the plays do to and with them. It is a view of Shakespeare seen through the lens of Max Weber. The disenchantment is that of the teller rather than that of the tale.

It is, however, possible to avoid seeing the early modern theater as an example, if not in part the source, of Western disenchantment, but then, I suppose, we'd also have to see it as somewhat less early *modern*, freeing it from the teleology the ubiquitous periodizing label presumes. Indeed, Jeffrey Knapp has energetically argued that what happens in the theater is less compensation than competition. The theater is not a response to loss but to inadequacy. It is not disenchanted at all. The players and their playwrights become a "kind of ministry" in themselves, "a means 'not to fight against [God's] word' but to save it from papists and preachers," as theater artists produce plays "intended and received as contributions to the cause of true religion."[22]

But if the compensatory model might be thought too easily to assume the sophisticated form of secularism it sets out to explain, Knapp's competitive model might be said to assume the enchantment it sets out to reclaim. Knapp interestingly reverses the usual focus on the anti-theatrical pamphlets to make visible and to take seriously the arguments made on the theater's behalf, but the competition between players and preachers seems far more likely to be, as was regularly said, a competition for audiences rather than for souls.[23] Although John Northbrooke's view of the commercial theaters as "a spectacle and schoole for all wickednesse and vice to be learned"[24] seems borderline hysterical, few, other than perhaps some interested playwrights, would have completely reversed the judgment to claim in any meaningful sense that plays were "godly enterprises."[25] The theaters were certainly not "the chappell of Satan," as Stephen Gosson said,[26] but neither were they the outbuildings of the temple of the Lord.

Knapp, however, unembarrassedly admits that religion—*as* religion— matters in Shakespeare, matters *to* Shakespeare, and he is appropriately unwilling to see it as something false or merely functional. But Knapp is more willing than I am to seek out Shakespeare's own religious beliefs, or more confident than I that he can identify what he finds, even if his evidence and my intuition in the end do not vary all that much. This book does in part explore what we know and mostly don't know about what Shakespeare believed, but it is more interested in how religion is presented in the plays and how the subject gets shaped by Shakespeare's imaginative engagement, inviting our own, than in anything the plays might tell us about Shakespeare's beliefs. It is not that I don't care what Shakespeare believed; it is that, as Chapter 2 argues, I don't think the plays or his known biography can tell us anything about that. I don't know what he believed, and I am convinced we can't know. Nonetheless, the renewed interest in Shakespeare's religion has at least forced Shakespeare scholars to think about religion as an essential aspect of early modern life and as a principal concern of Shakespeare himself, even if some of these scholars have been led to do so in large part by the very bardolatry that had initially concealed it.

Still, exactly how religion functions in the plays now seems the question, and the many recent studies offering (differing) suggestive answers may prove no more than how difficult that question is. It does seem clear that "the theatre in Elizabethan and Jacobean London" served, as Huston Diehl argued, as an "arena in which the disruptions, conflicts, and radical changes wrought by the Protestant Reformation are publicly explored."[27] However, the exploration is almost never concerned with the points of doctrine, the prerogatives of the Church, or the forms of worship that underwent change and often remained contested. Rather, the theater's engagement with the reforms and the debates they occasioned mostly takes place in an entirely different register, only as they have filtered down, almost always unremarked and usually unobserved, into the terms and forms of connection that mark our social world. Crises of belief in the plays are more likely to be provoked psychologically than doctrinally, functions not of soteriological uncertainty (*Hamlet* is perhaps the exception proving this rule; see Chapter 5) but of sexual insecurity (see almost every play); and if there is some analogy to be sensed between these, it is still only an analogy.[28] No doubt the sixteenth-century religious debates occupied Shakespeare's imagination, and arguably even helped shape it, but the most consequential evidence of his engagement with them is usually at several removes from their primary terms.

I understand that in this book I may have taken what might be thought the easy way out—or, more precisely, the easy way in. Where religion is closest to the surface is unsurprisingly at the level of religious identification, which basically accounts for the shape the lectures and now the book have taken. The readings work from the outside in, from public identity to the baffling inwardness of faith, from character and plot to the particularities of grammar, diction, and rhythm, while the order of the chapters proceeds almost exactly in the opposite direction, from the inside out: one on Shakespeare's own religion, one on his presentation of Catholics and Catholicism, one on Jews, Moors, and Turks in the two Venice plays, and a final chapter on literature's most famous Wittenberg dropout. The structure functions less as taxonomy than prompt, a means (one, of course, of many possible means) to engage the question of what religion is doing in these plays.

I am, at least in this introduction, more confident about saying what I think it is not doing in them. Religion does not mark the plays as sectarian or as sacramental. Since the reformers so insistently stressed *sola fide*, we might easily be tempted to hear something similar in *The Winter's Tale*: "It is required/You do awake your faith" (5.3.94–5). But it is Paulina not Paul who demands it of Leontes, and it is Shakespeare who asks it of us. The faith required in reading or seeing Shakespeare is clearly something different than the saving faith "that being quickened thereby we may liue eternally,"[29] although it is a faith that, as Jonson understood, may in some different sense allow Shakespeare to live "for all time." What is demanded from us is neither belief in God nor trust in His word, but only "that willing suspension of disbelief" in the fictions that Shakespeare has created.[30] Paulina's directive stipulates the terms of our covenant with Shakespeare, to which we assent as we enter the theater or as we open a playbook: he will create believable characters, and we will respond with our will to believe in what he has created.

Notes

1 Richard Wilson, *Will Power: Essays on Shakespearean Authority* (Detroit, MI: Wayne State University Press, 1993); David Wilburn, *Poetic Will: Shakespeare and the Play of Language* (Philadelphia: University of Pennsylvania Press,

1997); Lisa Freinkel, *Reading Shakespeare's Will: The Theology of Figure from Augustine to the Sonnets* (New York: Columbia University Press, 2002); Stephen Greenblatt, *Will in the World: How Shakespeare Became Shakespeare* (New York: W. W. Norton, 2004); James Shapiro, *Contested Will: Who Wrote Shakespeare?* (New York: Simon and Shuster, 2010); Tina Packer's 'Women of Will' is a two-person show about Shakespeare's female characters, performed in New York in 2013.

2 James, "The Will to Believe," in *The Will to Believe and Other Essays in Popular Philosophy* (New York: Longmans Green, 1896).

3 James, "The Will to Believe," 9.

4 Cf. Richard Hooker, "do wee not see the spirit every where in the scripture proveth matters of fayth, laboureth to confirme us in that which wee beleeve by thinges whereof wee have sensible knowledg?" in "A Learned and Comfortable Sermon on the certaintie and Perpetuitie of Faith in the Elect," in *The Folger Edition of the Works of Richard Hooker*, volume 5, ed. W. Speed Hill (Cambridge, MA: Harvard University Press, for the Folger Shakespeare Library, 1990), 70.

5 For an overview of the use of "confessionalism" in religious history, see Thomas A. Brady, "Confessionalization—The Career of a Concept," in *Confessionalization in Europe, 1555–1700*, eds. John M. Headley, Hans J. Hillerbrand, and Anthony J. Papalas (Burlington, VT: Ashgate, 2004), 1–20; and Joel F. Harrington and Helmut Walser Smith, "Confessionalization, Community, and State Building in Germany, 1555–1870," *Journal of Modern History* 69 (1997), 77–101.

6 Quoted in J. E. Neale, *Elizabeth I and her Parliaments, 1584–1601* (1958; New York: Norton, 1966), p. 424.

7 From "An Apologie of Raymond Sebond," in *The Essayes or Morall, Politike and Millitarie Discourses of Lo: Michaell de Montaigne*, trans. John Florio (London, 1603), sig. Ff8^v.

8 Haigh, *The Plain Man's Pathways to Heaven: Kinds of Christianity in Reformation England* (Oxford: Oxford University Press, 2007), 79.

9 Julia Lupton has made the useful point that "religion is not identical with culture." My claim here is only the obvious one that religion is often experienced both as culture and belief, that is, as individuals recognize various social practices and affiliations, and, usually unconsciously, assume certain intellectual habits and frames, that religious identification encourages, insists upon, or sometimes prohibits, as well as in the individual terms of faith. See her "The Religious Turn (to Theory) in Shakespeare Studies," *English Language Notes* 44 (2006), 146.

10 Ritson, *Remarks Critical and Illustrative on the Texts and Notes of the Last Edition of Shakespeare* (London, 1783), 188.

11 Dryden, "Preface," *All for Love, or The World Well Lost* (London, 1692), sig. B3^v.

12 The quotation from Voltaire appeared originally in his "Essai sur la poésie épique," and can be found translated in "A Shakespeare Journal,"

Yale French Studies 33.3 (1964), 5 (emphasis mine); Arthur Murphy, *Gray's-Inn Journal* (28 July 1753), quoted in *Shakespeare: The Critical Heritage: The Story of Shakespeare's Reputation*, vol. 4, ed. Brian Vickers, (New York and London: Routledge, 1976), 93; Morley, introduction to *As You Like It*, in *The Plays of Shakespeare*, ed. Henry Morley (New York: Doubleday and McClure, 1897), 5.

13 See his *Shakespeare: The Invention of the Human* (New York: Riverhead, 1998), 716 and p. xix.

14 For a sense of the debate, see Charles Taylor's magisterial *A Secular Age* (Cambridge, MA: Harvard University Press, 2007), which insists that secularity is not opposed to religion but is a historical development "from a society where belief in God is unchallenged and unproblematic, to one in which it is understood to be one option among others, and frequently not the easiest to embrace" (p. 3). In these terms, it is clear why its application to Shakespeare is problematic.

15 Santayana, "The Absence of Religion in Shakespeare," in *Selected Critical Writings of George Santayana, Volume 1*, ed. Norman Henfrey (Cambridge, Cambridge University Press, 1968), 60–71. The quotation appears on p. 69.

16 *The Gospel According to Shakespeare*, trans. Vittorio Montemaggi and Rachel Jacoff (Notre Dame, IN: University of Notre Dame Press, 2013), p. xi.

17 Goethe, quoted in *The Romantics on Shakespeare*, ed. Jonathan Bate (New York: Penguin, 1992), 71.

18 R. P. Blackmur, *Henry Adams*, ed. Veronica A. Makowsky (New York: Harcourt Brace Jovanovich, 1980), 315.

19 The loci classici for this idea may well be C. L. Barber's "The Family in Shakespeare's Development: Tragedy and Sacredness," in *Representing Shakespeare: New Psychoanalytic Essays*, eds. Murray M. Schwartz and Cop-pélia Kahn (Baltimore, MD: Johns Hopkins University Press, 1980), 188–202, which sees the theater appropriating the sacred; and Louis Montrose's "The Purpose of Playing: Reflections on Shakespearean Anthropology," *Helios* 7.2 (1979–80), 51–74. See also Stephen Greenblatt's *Shakespearean Negotiations: The Circulation of Social Energy in Renaissance England* (Berkeley and Los Angeles, CA: University of California Press, 1988), which talks about "the swerve from the sacred to the secular" as a function of "evacuation and transformed reiteration" (pp. 126–7).

20 Regina Mara Schwartz, *Sacramental Poetics at the Dawn of Secularism: When God Left the World* (Stanford, CA: Stanford University Press, 2008), 42.

21 Rushdie, "Is Nothing Sacred," in *Imaginary Homelands: Essays and Criticism 1981–1991* (New York: Penguin, 1992), 424. The idea seemingly derives from Pascal, *Pensées*, 425, though Pascal's oft-quoted "God-shaped vacuum" is not present in his French. Pascal, in any case, is developing an idea that probably goes back to Eccclesiastes 3:11.

22 Knapp, *Shakespeare's Tribe: Church, Nation, and Theater in Renaissance England* (Chicago and London: University of Chicago Press, 2002), 120, 9.

23 See the Lord Mayor's concern in 1592 that the appeal of plays drew "all sorts" in London "from their daylie resort vnto sermons & other Christian exercises," in E. K. Chambers, *The Elizabethan Stage* (Oxford: Clarendon Press, 1923), vol. 4, 307.

24 Chambers, *Elizabethan Stage*, vol. 4, 198.

25 Knapp, *Shakespeare's Tribe*, 2.

26 Chambers, *Elizabethan Stage*, vol. 4, 211.

27 Diehl, *Staging Reform, Reforming the Stage: Protestantism and Popular Theater in Early Modern England* (Ithaca, NY and London: Cornell University Press, 1997), 4.

28 See Claire McEachern's "Why Do Cuckolds Have Horns?" *Huntington Library Quarterly*, 71 (2008), 607–31 and her forthcoming *Believing in Shakespeare*, which brilliantly explore exactly this analogy between religious faith and the terms of faith in one another on which our social and emotional lives depend.

29 John Moore, *A Map of Mans Mortalitie* (London, 1617), sig. H3ᵛ; see also R. P., *The Cristall of Christianitie, or Looking Glasse of Gods Loue* (London, 1617), sig. D8ʳ: "A Christian...must constantly be perswaded that beleeuing in the Sonne of God, by this his faith, he shall liue eternally, and shall neuer perish."

30 Coleridge, *Biographia Literaria*, ed. George Watson (London: J. M. Dent, 1975), 169. See Richard C. McCoy, *Faith in Shakespeare* (New York: Oxford University Press, 2013), for a full account of the relationship between Coleridge's "poetic faith" and religious faith in our experience of Shakespeare's plays.

2
Shakespeare's Religion

> Though it is often said that we know very little about Shake-
> speare's life, it would be closer to the truth to say that we know
> quite a lot, but that what we know includes very little of what
> we should most like to know.
>
> Stanley Wells

The most enduring cliché of Shakespeare criticism is that of his
endurance. Ben Jonson's phrase, that he was "not of an age, but for
all time," introduced the trope of timelessness and universality that
would come to define him. But the qualities that have been identified as those which make him "OUR. EVER-LIVING POET," as
the dedication to the 1609 *Sonnets* claims, are not only those of his
superior artistic skill but also of his sympathetic psychological and
social imagination. He becomes the writer almost uniquely able to
free himself from his own historical moment, even as he is nourished
by it. Like Antony's "delights," the riches of his artistry are seen to
raise themselves "dolphin-like...above/The element they lived in"
(*Antony and Cleopatra*, 5.2.88–9). The workings of his imagination are
at least temporarily able to escape the constraints of the orthodoxies,
even of the controversies, that defined his age. His element—our
element—is history, but he seems, like the acrobatic dolphin, spec-
tacularly able to rise and see above it.

Keats would call this power *Negative Capability*, the quality of mind
necessary to "form a Man of Achievement, especially in Literature,
and which Shakespeare possessed so enormously."[1] Shakespeare
seemingly remains unfettered by the structures of thought that surrounded him to see and write the world in his capacious and committed disinterestedness. An unsigned essay in the *Edinburgh Review*

of 1866 saw Shakespeare as "a man of true nobility of soul," who, unlike his countrymen, who were "lurching between Geneva and Rome," refused the partisanship of contemporary religion: "Shakespeare became impatient with the harbour to which, he was moored by accidents of birth, and set sail for the wider ocean of humanity."[2] Almost forty years earlier, Thomas Carlyle had already insisted: "Shakespeare is no sectarian; to all he deals with equity and mercy, because he knows all and his heart is wide enough for all."[3] Shakespeare rises above any one religion by becoming the God of all religions, dealing "with equity and mercy," all-knowing, and with an apparently infinite capacity to love.

But recently Shakespeare has come to seem a sectarian after all. For the first decade of the twenty-first century, virtually all of the energy of Shakespeare scholarship, as almost all other existing modes of critical engagement had begun to feel more or less exhausted, seemed directed at deciding exactly where his confessional loyalties lay. For a time, the question of whether Shakespeare was a Catholic seemed to be about the only thing worth debating.[4] Certainly it was the only thing about Shakespeare that would find its way into the popular press, although admittedly the question "Was Shakespeare a Catholic?" often seemed a welcome relief from "Was Shakespeare the Earl of Oxford?" and indeed is somewhat more likely to be answered in the affirmative. Suddenly the focus was not just on religion but on *his* religion, and scholars sought the signs of its animating history as it has left traces in his plays or in the slim biographical records that have survived.

Perhaps this was because a dissident Shakespeare is for us more appealing, perhaps more useful, than the Shakespeare who for so long has been co-opted to articulate and guarantee the norms of a dominant culture. Or perhaps it was because, as various post-structuralisms have threatened us with "the death of the author," we feel the need to reconstitute this most precious author from within, in his most intimate and authentic dimension. Or perhaps it was because our own recent history has so dramatically refused the secular end the Enlightenment had posited for it, sometimes murderously reminding us of the tenacity of faith in human culture.

Each of these possible motives no doubt says more about us than about Shakespeare (as usually the focus of Shakespeare scholarship does). Still, for whatever reasons, religion has been enthusiastically returned to the calculus of value that measures our interest in Shakespeare, with a new near-orthodoxy that says Shakespeare was, if not a believing Catholic, at the very least sympathetic to aspects of Catholicism and to the values of the English people before the nation was "at controversie."[5] There is no evidence for Shakespeare as a recusant, but Gary Taylor has argued that "for much of his life Shakespeare was a church papist," one of those who, as John Earle said, "kneels with the Congregation, but prayes by himself."[6] Or maybe it was only his father, John, who held to the traditional faith, with Shakespeare himself, as Stephen Greenblatt has argued, "haunted by the spirit of his Catholic father," even as his own faith lapsed.[7] Or perhaps Shakespeare, as we have always thought, was indeed not only a conforming Protestant but also a believing one, although one for whom the pre-Reformation past, possibly recalled in sonnet 73's "Bare ruined choirs, where late the sweet birds sang," represented a yearned-for coherence that had shattered in the volatile post-Reformation world in which he lived.[8]

Though each of these seems a plausible version of Shakespeare's religion, how would we know which, if any, is true? What evidence might have significant probative value? What exactly can that evidence prove about something as inward as belief? I don't have many new facts to add to the discussion, but I am interested mainly in what we have made of the ones we have. There is, of course, his "professione of fayth," the document in which "Wm Shakspear" commits his soul to the "lovynge and greate God and toe hys gloriouse sonne Jesus." The preamble is a conventional Protestant formula, and the document goes on appealingly to match the promise of Matthew 23:37 to the homely realities of the rural life into which Shakespeare was born. While he admits that he is "full of Synne" and not "worthye offe thye grace," he trusts that God will "cherishe usse like the sweete Chickeene thatte under the coverte offe herre spreadynge Wings Receyves herre lyttle Broode and hovering oerre themme keepes themme harmlesse ande in safetye."[9]

Still, at most this might establish what Shakespeare believed on his deathbed. But it cannot even do that. Alas, the document is an all-too-apparent forgery by William Henry Ireland from the 1790s.[10] That it was ever accepted as authentic testifies far more to our desire to know what Shakespeare believed than to the skill of the forger, whose implausible understanding of early modern spelling habits seems primarily to assume their almost invariant retention of an unstressed final "e." It proves *our* will to believe rather than Shakespeare's. No document survives to satisfy our desire, but the absence has done little to quench the yearning for it. If anything it has made it more intense.

As Shakespeare's religion has returned to the calculus of value surrounding his writing (rather than its absence being in some sense a measure of its worth), scholars have mined the inconveniently less explicit legitimate records to determine what Ireland took for granted and would have verified through his own invention. In fact, Shakespeare nowhere says anything explicitly about what he believes, but even if he did it would tell us only what he believed when he said it or what he was willing to say about what he believed. Nevertheless, the existing historical record is suggestive. Or is it maddening?

* * * * *

It is often stated, for example, that his mother's family was staunchly Catholic, though the claim may be both less controversial and consequential than it might first appear (depending, I suppose, what one means by "staunchly"), since almost everyone of Mary Arden's generation would have had parents who were raised in the traditional religion.[11] It does seem clear that her father, Shakespeare's grandfather, had lived and died a Catholic. His will, dated 24 November 1556, in addition to leaving Mary ten marks and all his "lande in Wilmecote cawlide Asbyes and the crop apone the ground," bequeathed his soul, in an unmistakably Catholic formula, "to Allmyghtye God and to our bleside Laydye Sent Marye and to all the holye companye of heven."[12]

But for Mary's own generation, when the assertion of the family's Catholicism might have some greater scholarly significance, it is harder to tell if it is true. We do know that Edward Arden of Park Hall (about twenty-five miles from Stratford-upon-Avon), a prominent Catholic, was executed in 1583 for his putative involvement with a threat to shoot the Queen by his deranged son-in-law John Somerville.[13] Too much, however, may have been made of this. There is no direct evidence to establish that the Ardens of Park Hall were related to Shakespeare's mother's family (though it seems likely the families were distantly related),[14] but the family litmus test would prove to be ambivalent in any case. Alexander Webbe, the husband of Mary's sister Margaret, seemingly was a Protestant; at the very least their son, his wife, and two of their children emigrated in 1626 with Puritan dissenters to Massachusetts.[15] And while Mary herself was almost certainly baptized and raised a Catholic (given her father's will and having been born in the 1530s before the reform was widespread), we have no evidence at all of her own beliefs as an adult.

Her first child, Joan, was baptized by Roger Dyos on 15 September 1558 in the Roman rite, and died soon after. But if the baptism would have saved the infant's soul, the form of the ceremony doesn't tell us anything certain about her mother's faith. The baptism could not have been otherwise. Queen Mary still ruled, having ordered the traditional forms of worship to be restored after the reforms initiated late in the reign of her father, Henry VIII, and intensified in the reign of her half-brother, Edward.

A little over two months after Joan's baptism, however, Queen Mary was dead. Elizabeth succeeded to the English throne on 17 November, with the formal coronation on 15 January of 1559. With Elizabeth now queen, the liturgical reforms undone by Mary were officially restored, though the Protestantizing of worship in Stratford-upon-Avon generally seems to have been embraced less than enthusiastically, as indeed was the case at the first go-round. In 1537, Hugh Latimer, in a letter accepting Thomas Cromwell's recommendation of Anthony Barker to serve as warden of the collegiate church, had referred to the small market town as "that blind end of my diocese,"[16] and in 1559 the market town wasn't much more zealous.

Nonetheless, the town corporation forced Dyos's removal, voting to withhold his salary to encourage his departure after he refused either to conform or to resign, and early in 1560 he was replaced as vicar by John Bracegirdle ("Bretchgirdle"). Bracegirdle had received his MA in 1547 at Christ Church, Oxford, which had been founded by Henry VIII as part of an intended reform of both the diocese and the University, and was conveniently unmarried, so his appointment would not have offended Catholics who disapproved of married clergy. When he officiated at the baptism of William Shakespeare on

26 April 1564 (6 May, in our calendar, as we often forget, since England didn't adopt the Gregorian calendar until 1752), the vicar would have conducted a ceremony "ministered in the English tongue" and conducted according to the Prayer Book of 1559. The ceremony, which omitted the anointing of the child with chrism, reveals its Protestantism in no small part in its call upon the newly baptized child "to heare Sermons" as soon as that was possible.[17] But that can tell us no more about Mary's faith than can the baptism of Joan. The form of the baptism in both cases was not something she could have chosen, but in whatever form it would not have been something she would have been likely to deny her infant.

The reformed service was obviously intended by those who established it to have a different sacramental meaning than the Catholic version. Baptism became now the sign and seal of the infant's incorporation into the community of the faithful rather than an instrument of spiritual transformation, a "public" rather than a "private" sacrament, but it isn't at all certain, as John Cox has astutely observed, that the family would have recognized it so.[18] The different baptismal rites seem firm evidence only of the pragmatic truth of *cuius regio, eius religio*. They tell us no more about Mary Arden's faith than does the fact that she was buried in the graveyard of Holy Trinity Church. In any case, as a post-partum mother she would not have been present at the baptism of either child. New mothers stayed at home, and appeared at church only after a month for a ceremony known as the "Churching of Women."[19]

There are at least a few records bearing directly on the religion of Shakespeare's father. Having been born about 1530, John Shakespeare, like his wife, was raised in a Catholic family and grew up in a community that was recognizably slow to embrace any change to the established religion. Although the reforming Latimer was appointed bishop of Worcester in 1537, his tenure lasted only two years with little evidence of any lasting impact upon the diocese. With Latimer's departure, and clear evidence of the Crown's desire to slow the pace of reform, the citizenry seems happily to have returned to its traditional ways. Yet with Henry's death in 1547 and Edward VI's accession to the throne, an aggressive program of reform was initiated, which resulted in significant institutional and devotional change, only some of which could be turned back when the Catholic Mary came to the throne in 1553. What John Shake-speare felt about any of this is unknown, but as a man of obvious civic commitment and entrepreneurial energy he was certainly aware of what was happening around him, which might well have made him cautious about overtly committing to any faith in such a vertiginous world.

Nonetheless, twice in 1592 he is named in recusancy certificates for Warwickshire. Technically "recusancy," though it has become a term for Catholic resistance, refers to "all such as refuse obstinately to resort to Church," in the language of the articles attached to the proclamation of 18 October 1591 that established the commission to undertake the local survey,[20] and was used to define Puritan dissenters as well as Catholic. It seems clear, however, that this particular proclamation was mainly motivated by fear of a Spanish invasion and concerned with the activities of English Catholics who might, as the document says, "acknowledge any kind of obedience to the Pope, or to the King of Spain."[21] The commission established for Warwickshire filed its reports first at Easter 1592 (only the preliminary draft of this survives) and again at Michaelmas. In both, John Shakespeare is named as one of those who was regularly absent from church, though the reason is given in the later certificate as "feare of processe for Debtte."[22]

It is possible that this was, as some scholars have claimed, merely a convenient cloak behind which to hide his principled dissent, but it is worth noting that the autumn return carefully distinguishes categories of non-attendance: 1) those who "willfully persist in their recusancy"; 2) "dangerous and seditious papists and recusants...now either beyond the seas or vagrant within this realm"; 3) "recusants...either dwelling in other counties or gone out of this country upon their just occasions, or to lurk unknown in other countries"; 4) those who "are thought to forbear the church for debt or from fear of process, or for some other worse faults, or for age, sickness, or impotency of body"; and 5) those who had conformed or "else have promised to conform themselves and to go to the church."[23] John Shakespeare is listed in category four, differentiated from those who "wilfully persist in their recusancy" and indeed, as Robert Bearman notes, is "included in the one category of five designed to cover those who were *not* recusants."[24] Furthermore, the common claim that recusants regularly invoked "fear of process" to hide their Catholicism is belied, at least in Warwickshire, by the fact that fewer than one percent offered this explanation, and the commission of prominent local justices would have had little reason to disguise the truth about their neighbors and less not to know it.[25]

Nonetheless, John Shakespeare might have tried to conceal his faith. We don't know if fear of facing his creditors motivated his failure to attend church, reflecting a downturn in his business fortunes, or if that was merely "the stereotyped excuse with nonconforming Papists," as Richard Simpson long ago claimed, however less than truly stereotypical it in fact seems to have been.[26] Might it have been both in John Shakespeare's case? All we know for sure is that he did not attend church regularly; why he didn't can only be conjectural.

But another document might be thought to tip the balance: the so-called "Spiritual Testament." Allegedly found in 1757 among the roof-tiles in the Shakespeare family house on Henley Street in Stratford by a bricklayer, Joseph Moseley, the pamphlet is a Catholic profession of faith in fourteen articles attested to by John Shakespeare. The original document is lost, but a manuscript copy, made by John Jordan, a Stratford wheelwright and amateur antiquarian, who claimed to have been given the document by Moseley, is presently in the Birmingham Reference Library.[27] Edmond Malone published a version in his Shakespeare edition of 1790.[28] In the testament, John Shakespeare pledges his faith to the "Catholic, Roman, and Apostolic Church," offers a prayer to be delivered from the "pains and torments" of purgatory, and appoints "the glorious and ever Virgin Mary," along with St Winifred, as "chief Executress" of the will.

Unquestionably this is a Catholic testament, and the common Victorian certitude that the whole thing was an obvious forgery[29] was essentially disproved in 1923, when it was discovered that the Stratford formulary, except for its first two and half articles, followed phrase for phrase the form of a spiritual testament drawn up in the 1570s by Cardinal Borromeo, the zealous counter-Reformation Archbishop of Milan, and then circulated through Europe. Since the dependence of John Shakespeare's testament upon the Borromeo template seems not to have been known until 1923 when

Father Herbert Thurston found a printed Spanish version dated 1661 in the British Library,[30] it is very tempting to conclude that the document found in 1757 is authentic. Two printed English versions of the Borromeo testament, one from 1635 and one from 1638, have since been found.[31]

But is the religious formulary, therefore, proof of John Shakespeare's faith? "Maybe" is probably the best answer we can give. The most compelling argument for its authenticity is on the grounds of probability; that is, that for it to be a forgery someone (Jordan?) had to have come across a copy (almost certainly defective, lacking the first two and a half articles) of the English version of the Borromeo testament, of which otherwise there was no record until Thurston's discovery in 1923, and to have recognized the opportunity it provided to create a significant "Shakespeare" document. It is, of course, not impossible that this is what happened. Indeed, as we have seen, it was at almost the same time that this discovery was made public that William Henry Ireland was bold enough to forge a Protestant testimony of faith for John Shakespeare's son.[32] But it seems simpler to accept it for what it claims to be,[33] and yet that would demand the extraordinary coincidence, as Robert Bearman reminds us, that the sole existing manuscript copy of the Borromeo testament "just happened to be subscribed to by the father of perhaps the most famous of all Englishmen."[34]

In either case, it is the worrisome singularity of the document upon which the argument for either its authenticity or its illegitimacy rests that undermines it. Is it more probable that an amateur Stratford antiquarian (who, it should be noted, was not a Catholic) found an English translation of the Borromeo testament, of which no other English version was known until 1966, and that he decided to forge evidence of John Shakespeare's enduring Catholicism? Or that a manuscript version of the Borromeo testament, of which no other example is known, reached John Shakespeare, and that he, or someone acting for him, filled in his name in the blanks of the formulary to confirm his Catholicism? I don't know. Each seems to me almost equally *im*probable, but one of these must be true.

Some of the doubts surrounding the testament might have been answered had the original manuscript that Malone saw not disappeared. The final article, for example, says that it is "signed with

mine own hand," but John Shakespeare never signed any documents, marking them usually with a drawn compass.[35] It would help
to know what was there on the page. We do know that the first two
and a half articles in Jordan's manuscript and printed by Malone in
an appendix (see note 28) are a clumsy forgery. They are theologically inappropriate for the rest of the document, with its very Protestant hope to be saved "through the only merits of Jesus Christ my
saviour and redeemer," and marked also by the odd quotation from
Hamlet: "cut off in the blossoms of my sin."[36] We do know that
Malone himself, having at first been "perfectly satisfied" that the
testament itself was "genuine,"[37] later wrote: "I certainly was mis-
taken; for I have since obtained documents that clearly prove it
could not have been the composition of any one of our poet's family; as will be fully shewn in his Life."[38] Malone, however, never
completed his *Life of Shakespeare*, and, after his death, James Boswell,
attempting to finish it from Malone's notes, announced that he had
not "been able to discover this documentary evidence."[39]

There is also the oddity in the document itself that in Article
twelve, the testator, "John Shakespeare," asks all his "dear friends,
parents, and kinsfolks" to pray for him, even though his own parents
had died well before the Borromeo testaments were composed (and
the argument that has been offered, that "parents" merely means
relatives, is vitiated by the presence of what would then be the tautological noun "kinsfolk"). In fact, the phrase exactly duplicates the
wording of the surviving formularies, so whoever wrote in the name
John Shakespeare, maybe even his son William or, perhaps, an
eighteenth-century forger, merely wasn't paying close enough attention to notice that this article as written didn't apply in this particular case, or, perhaps, the testament had belonged to a different John
Shakespeare to whom it did (another John Shakespeare, a shoe-
maker, did live in Stratford for a time), or...we could go on
speculating.

But even if it is real—that is, even if it is the Spiritual Testament
subscribed to by John Shakespeare, William's father—one might
reasonably wonder why it was in the roof. Those who defend its
authenticity usually insist it was hidden there because John wanted
to be sure that it would not be found by Protestant authorities in hot
pursuit of recusant Catholics. In the aftermath of the Somerville

plot, many Warwickshire Catholics, according to Thomas Wilkes, a clerk of the Privy Council, "greatly work upon the advantage of clearing their house of all shows of suspicion."[40] The testament itself, however, says that the document is to be "often" read by the "devout person who will make use of this spiritual writing" and kept "always with him to have it ready on all occasions." And at his death, it was to be buried with him, which might serve to account for the fact that almost none have survived.[41] If the formularies were indeed intended, in Alexandra Walsham's phrase, as "an act of defiance, an assertion of identity, and a self-consciously pious gesture,"[42] its presence in the roof might, then, actually be evidence *against* it having confessional significance for John Shakespeare. Perhaps it is authentic, but was preserved only because he had at some time merely ceased to care about it.

There is no way to know about any of this, and the undeserved confidence with which the case has usually been argued from both sides inevitably suggests the special pleading of each. There is no way to establish if the Spiritual Testament is authentic and, even if we could, there is no way to determine what the document represented for John Shakespeare. We should at the very least remind ourselves that John Shakespeare baptized his last seven children and buried two of them in the rites of the reformed Church, and that in his role as borough Chamberlain he was responsible "for defasyng ymages in ye chapell,"[43] as well as "taking doune" its "rood loft" and erecting a communion table to satisfy the expectations of the reformed in Stratford or maybe only of the Protestant bishop of the diocese. Some years later, as deputy-bailiff, John Shakespeare would agree to the sale of the copes, manuaries, and vestments of the guild chapel "to the use of the Chamber."

Maybe all of this is nothing more than evidence that John Shakespeare was willing to enact his civic responsibilities and to conform to the state religion, as were many Catholics, who went to church but continued to believe in the traditional faith that many in England did not abandon when, with the official break from Rome, the Church *in* England became the Church *of* England. Most people probably did what they had to do to live comfortably within their local communities and left the divisive matters of doctrine and faith to their private relations with God. Maybe. It seems clear that in many cases private belief and public worship were held separate, suggesting how inadequate—even inappropriate—doctrinal labels are.

But even if we could be certain that the Spiritual Testament established that John Shakespeare lived and died "an unworthy member of the Holy Catholick religion," as the transcribed formulary's first article would attest, it would still tell us nothing certain about *William* Shakespeare's faith. Perhaps all we can say with confidence about William is that he, as Park Honan puts it, "was raised in the shadow of the old faith."[44] But Honan's formulation is remarkably, though also responsibly, cautious. At least depending on what one thinks cast that shadow, it commits itself to very little and to nothing that is in dispute.

Certainly Shakespeare grew up in a world in which the traditional religion still must have exerted some theological and affective claims on the community in which he lived, and yet he would have had little, if any, experience of Catholic forms of worship. What he *believed* must elude us, but he was baptized and buried in the reformed religion, as were his children; he was never cited for recusancy, he lived for a time with a Huguenot family in London, after 1596 he quotes most often from the Geneva Bible (even quoting on occasion from its marginalia, so it was a bible he had read rather than only heard), and his plays held the stage and appeared in increasing numbers on the bookstalls with no sign of having raised any official concern about their religious commitments.[45] Perhaps it is true, as the Anglican divine Richard Davies noted, that Shakespeare "dyed a Papist,"[46] but there is no firm evidence that he ever lived as one.

Some scholars have sought that evidence in the 1581 will of Alexander Hoghton, a Catholic living near Preston in Lancashire. A "William Shakeshafte" is among eleven "servants" who are left an annuity, and who is one of two recommended by Hoghton to his younger brother Thomas to be taken into service or helped "to some good master." The name of course is suggestive, and a previous clause in the will leaves "intrumentes belonginge to mewsyckes & all manner of playe clothes" to Hoghton's brother, "yf he be mynded to keppe & doe keppe players," leading some to speculate that the then seventeen-year-old Shakespeare was a member of an acting company based at Hoghton Tower in the recusant community, which some have over enthusiastically claimed as "the secret headquarters of the English Counter-Reformation."[47] But Shakeshafte was a common Lancashire name, not obviously interchangeable with Shakespeare, in spite of both the known fluidity of spelling in the period and the iconic similarity of shafts and spears. More tellingly, the Shakeshafte who is a beneficiary of Hoghton's will—and of his good will in the recommendation—seems more likely to be someone far better known to Hoghton and his family than the young Shakespeare who could only have recently arrived at the Hoghton household in Lancashire and who would very soon return to Warwickshire to marry in 1582 (and for whom the payment of the annuity if he were indeed a player would at the very least prove difficult). None of this disproves that Hoghton's beneficiary was William Shakespeare, but the evidence on offer hardly proves he is and tells us nothing, in any case, about what "William Shakeshafte" believed beyond what might be assumed from the fact of his Catholic employer.

William *Shakespeare* did, however, leave his own will, which begins with an expression of faith—and this will is undeniably genuine.

> In the name of God Amen I William Shakespeare...in perfect health & memorie god be praysed doe make & Ordayne this my last will & testament in manner & forme followeing: That ys to saye ffirst I Comend my Soule into the handes of god my Creator hoping & assuredlie beleeving through thonelie merittes of Jesus Christe my Saviour to be made p[ar]taker of lyfe everlastynge, And my bodye to the Earthe whereof yt ys made.[48]

This is as close as we can get to an expression of his own belief, and might well be taken as conclusive evidence, *pace* Davies, that, however he lived, he died a Protestant. While historians have usefully warned about the dangers in attempting to derive confessional loyalties from will preambles,[49] here there is an unmistakable Protestant marker: "through thonlie merittes of Jesus Christe." This is the defining *solus Christus* theme of Protestantism in which salvation is possible only through unmerited grace made available by the redemptive sacrifice of Christ. While Christians of any sort could commend themselves to God "by meritte of whose passion I wholly trust to be saved,"[50] in the words of a Suffolk will, it is the insistence on the unique efficaciousness of Christ's sacrifice for salvation that marks the formula in Shakespeare's will as Protestant (and marks at least the first article of John Shakespeare's "Spiritual Testament" as a forgery). As Christopher Marsh has argued: "the word 'only' carried huge force and was widely considered to express reformist attitudes when used in association with faith in Jesus Christ."[51]

The preamble to the will, however, may tell us far less than we might hope about Shakespeare's faith, since the wording turns out to be entirely formulaic. A book of legal forms reissued the year before Shakespeare's death includes as one of its templates, the almost identical preamble: "in the name of God Amen...sicke of bodie but of good and perfect memory (God be praised)...First I commend my soule into the handes of God my maker, hoping assuredly through the onely merites of Jesus Christ my Saviour to be made partaker of life euerlasting. And I commende my body to the earth whereof it is made."[52]

Even when we think we have a window into Shakespeare's soul it turns out still we only see through a glass darkly. Perhaps the will does show that Shakespeare died a Protestant; the conventionality of the phrasing says nothing one way or the other about whether he believed in what it asserted. But Catholics, of course, believed in Jesus Christ too, and the "only," of such "huge force," as Marsh put it, in the mid sixteenth century, may itself have become merely conventional by 1616 and have little if any theological import.[53]

Perhaps the will's unusual silence on funeral arrangements, with nothing more specific than commending his body to the earth, suggests his alienation from the parish church where he would be buried. His friend and colleague, John Heminge, in contrast, wrote in his will: "And my body I Commit to the earth to be buried in Christian manner in the parrish Church of Mary Aldenmanbury in London" and specified that his "funeral may be in decent and Comely manner performed in the Evening, without any vaine pompe or Cost therein to be bestowed," while the other editor of the First Folio, Henry Condell, less specifically, committed his body "to the Earth to be decentlie buried in the night tyme in such parishe where yt shall please God to call me."[54] Shakespeare, however, makes no reference whatsoever to his funeral. Do we have, then, even in the unelaborated Protestant formula, another hint of Shakespeare's crypto-Catholicism, or at least of his disaffection from the reformed

Church? Or might it be that Shakespeare, knowing full well to which parish it would please God to call him, and how prominent he was in that community, was sufficiently confident about the funeral arrangements to leave them unspecified in his will? Might this be evidence, then, not of his estrangement from the Church but of his comfort and confidence in it?

Again, it is impossible to know, as it is impossible to know what to make of the evidence of his daughter Susanna being cited along with twenty others in May of 1606 for not taking communion that Easter, an offence at most times likely to go unremarked but which in the aftermath of the Gunpowder Plot was included in an act designed to identify and punish "persons popishly affected."[55] Is this certain evidence of her Catholicism (or of her father's), or merely of the bad timing of her laxity, especially in light of the fact that the case was eventually dismissed, and of the clear Protestantism of her husband, whom she married the following year?

The problem of deciding whether Shakespeare (or his father) was a Catholic or a Protestant is not just a problem of inadequate or inconclusive evidence. It is as much a terminological difficulty as an evidentiary one. Sharp confessional differences blur in the bricolage of religious belief and pietistic practice that developed in the wake of the multiple shifts of religion and rule in Tudor England. For any individual, faith and practice may not align, and familial and local relationships might well, in any case, complicate one's confessional commitments. A neighbor may be a Catholic (or a Protestant) but is, nonetheless, a neighbor on whom one must sometime depend, and may even esteem, regardless of confessional loyalty. And even for a committed Protestant, the near certainty that one's grandparents, anyhow, would have been Catholics must have occasionally unsettled the confidence that justification always came by faith alone. "Thynke you to be saued, more then your parentes, or do you iudge them already condemned?" sneeringly asked the Catholic polemicist Miles Huggard in 1556 of his more zealous countrymen.[56]

Religious identities in early modern England, as we have learned, are characteristically far more eclectic and unstable than the polarized master categories of "Catholic" and "Protestant" allow.[57] James Shapiro has said sensibly that "except for a small minority at one doctrinal extreme or other, those labels failed to capture the layered nature of what Elizabethans, from the queen on down, actually believed."[58] But the evidentiary problem won't quite go away. While what Shapiro says is almost certainly true, it is as much to the point also to note that it is impossible for us to *know* what anyone in the period "actually believed." We may know what they did or even what they said, but what they held in their hearts remains hidden to us. This limit marks the inescapable epistemological problem of the inquiry, and perhaps is the sign that it is somewhat misconstrued. Shakespeare may have had, as his Richard II says, "thoughts of things divine" (5.5.12), but we have no access to these, and cannot know, in any case, how "intermixed" these might be with the sorts of "scruples" (i.e. doubts) Richard admits.

Shakespeare's faith cannot be recovered. Probably no one's can who isn't committed to demonstrating or explaining it. We can speculate about what he believed, trying to tease it out of the patchy historical record and the puzzling evidence of his writings. But it must remain merely a speculation. The historical record allows us nothing more. What it provides is fragmentary and inconclusive. Facts pop up, but they are the accidental survivors of history, and their significance attenuates as each is cut off by time and circumstance from the connective tissue of dailyness that might supply it with motivation and meaning. Isolated they become enigmatic texts in need of interpretation, vulnerable to hermeneutic limitation and our longing for presence.

And if Shakespeare's faith does not clearly emerge from the desultory narrative of his familial and personal history, it is no more evident in his literary texts. Although their gaps and ambiguities might be meaningful, unlike the inadvertent ones of history, which merely frustrate, they no better communicate a theological coherence or religious commitment that history denies us. Shakespeare's faith is no more legible in his poems and plays, but the literary texts, in their greater linguistic and formal density, are arguably (for better and worse) more responsive to our desire. They allow us more interpretive space as his language swells with our attention, absorbing our interests and our own histories. In the absence of an archive of non-literary writing that might reveal the inner Shakespeare, we have sought him in his writing.[59] "With this key/Shakespeare unlock'd his heart," Wordsworth would write in reference to the sonnets,[60] but the complete works have become a set of keys to open what Shakespeare had refused to make public and what history had locked away.

But there is too much writing, with too many thoughts and too many feelings. How do we differentiate what Shakespeare himself felt or believed from what Shakespeare thought could be experienced or might be believed by others? Should the jealous Othello be taken as evidence that Shakespeare was himself jealous or merely of the fact that he was capable of imagining jealousy? Even Malone suspected "that the author, at some period in his life, had been *perplexed* with doubts," though he realized the danger of the critical procedure: "by the same mode of reasoning, it may be said, he might be proved to have stabbed his friend, or to have had a *thankless* child."[61] No one would say, I assume, that at "some period in his life" Shakespeare must have contemplated murder because he so vividly can portray Macbeth's "horrible imaginings," which "unfix [his] hair" and make his "seated heart knock at [his] ribs" (1.3.139, 136–7). Which characters give voice to what Shakespeare had experienced or what he believed? Richard III? Of course not. Timon? Certainly no. Isabella or Cleopatra? Falstaff, or Coriolanus, or any of the many Antonios?

Did Shakespeare himself believe that "As flies to wanton boys are we to th' gods./They kill us for their sport" (*King Lear*, 4.1.38–9); or did he believe that "There is special providence in the fall of a sparrow" (*Hamlet*, 5.2.197–8)? Certainly we have to avoid the circularity of identifying the lines that we think point to what Shakespeare himself believed by referring to what we have already decided he did believe and then seeing the rest as the result of his keen observation and skillful artistry. But often that is what we have done. However, the complex relationship between what a character is saying and what Shakespeare thought may be impossible to unravel, not least because inevitably some other character has said the opposite. Near the end of *King Lear*, Gloucester replies as enthusiastically as he can manage to one of Edgar's many sententious formulations, "And that's true too" (5.2.11). At least it is as true as any of the various other things that Edgar has thought, and, anyway, even Gloucester's conciliatory line is "true" only for the Folio *Lear*; it is absent from the 1608 Quarto.

The extraordinary range of human emotion, thought, and experience that Shakespeare portrays, embedded in language almost uniquely interpretable, would allow almost anything to be claimed for Shakespeare himself. Indeed almost everything *has* been claimed about him—in terms of his occupational history, sexual orientation, political commitments, personality, as well as his religious beliefs. The limitations of taking what characters say as evidence of what Shakespeare personally felt, thought, or experienced (as opposed to what Shakespeare understood as what human beings might plausibly feel, think, or experience) must be obvious enough. It is impossible to know when the plays' religious vocabulary might be ventriloquizing an idea or belief of its author and when not. We might well notice that Helena is disguised as "Saint Jacques' pilgrim... [w]ith sainted vow" (*All's Well That Ends Well*, 3.4.4,7), but pointedly that is not what she is in the play, nor can its Catholic reference serve as any clear signpost to what Shakespeare is either. Reading fiction as autobiography misconstrues the basic idea of imagination, though arguably reading autobiography as autobiography does too.

If we are going to find Shakespeare's religion then, perhaps we should look for it in the deep structure of his writing, that is, not at what characters say (precisely because they are characters) but where Shakespeare consciously—or, better, unconsciously—finds the language he gives them. A character in Jane Austen's *Mansfield Park* claims credibly that everyone is "familiar with Shakespeare...from one's earliest years. His celebrated passages are quoted by every body; they are in half the books we open, and we all talk Shakespeare," but in Shakespeare's world the same could have been said with even less fear of contradiction about the Bible. They all talked it. One might, therefore, look to the inevitable substratum of biblical language that appears in the plays to tell us something about Shakespeare's faith, especially when that language, however certainly the word of God, in its various renditions into English could be marked by sharp confessional inflections that might be seen to register the divisions in the Christian community.

The remarkable density of biblical allusion in his writing leaves no doubt that Shakespeare regularly consulted or at least proficiently recalled his Bible, but just what "his" Bible was is not so easily established, still less what that might mean.[62] Scholars have identified hundreds of references, which testify, unsurprisingly, to the fact that Shakespeare knew the Bible well.[63] Familiarity, of course, was almost inevitable in a culture that officially held that "Holy Scriptures containeth all things necessary to salvation,"[64] and formally ensured access for the faithful with an annual schedule of scriptural readings. The Old Testament would be read through once a year, with the exception of "certain bokes and Chapiters, whiche bee least edifying, and might best be spared," as it said in the 1549 Book of Common Prayer; the New Testament was read three times, "except the Apocalypse, out of which there are only certain proper Lessons appointed upon divers feasts"; and the full book of Psalms was read once every month.[65] Church attendance, however, was required only on Sundays and holy days, so only the most diligent churchgoers would hear the full cycle of readings—and nothing, in any case, could be mandated about the attention of those who were in attendance.

But all who listened would have heard the scriptures in the English of the Great Bible first issued in 1539, which was used consistently in churches until the 1570s, when the Bishops' Bible, published originally in 1568 and substantially revised in 1572, came into general use (although some provincial churches kept the Great Bible they already owned). The Psalms read in the liturgy never changed from their Great Bible form. The 1572 Bishops' Bible printed its new translation side-by-side with the Great Bible psalter, identifying the earlier version as "The translation vsed in common prayer," and subsequent editions of the Bishops' Bible printed only the prayer book's Great Bible version.

These translations provided the words Shakespeare would have heard at services when he was present and listening, if indeed he was present and listening. The popular Geneva translation was published in 1560, and regularly reprinted in various forms and formats for another hundred years, but was never formally read in church. A "Catholic" Bible was not available in English until 1582 when the New Testament was published at Rheims (the Old Testament was not published until 1609/10 at Douai), and though officially proscribed it was available, if only in William Fulke's edition of 1589 designed to refute its authority.[66]

As the different English editions were ideologically differentiated by particular translations and often by marginal commentary, it is tempting to use this as another window into Shakespeare's soul, evidence of confessional commitments that seem otherwise hidden. But bibles for most people were merely bibles. Even Archbishop Laud can be found quoting from the very Geneva translation that he had ordered suppressed.[67] Shakespeare at times quotes from a Bishops' translation, remembers psalms as they were translated in the Great Bible, follows the Geneva wording, and on a few occasions seems to be thinking of the Counter-Reformation Rheims version, as in Parolles's invocation of the "the house with the narrow gate...too little for pomp to enter" (*All's Well That Ends Well*, 4.5.50–2), which follows Rheims's Matthew (7:13), rather than the Geneva's or Bishops' "streighte gate."[68] Even in a single play, Shakespeare remembers different translations. In *2 Henry IV*, Mistress Quickly urges Falstaff and Doll to "bear with another's confirmities" (2.4.57), mangling the Geneva Bible's version of Romans 15:1, which maintains that the strong "ought to beare the infirmities of the weake" rather than their "fraylnes," as the Bishops' Bible urges; while the new King's cold injunction to Falstaff to "[k]now the grave doth gape/For thee thrice wider than for other men" (5.5.53–4) echoes the Bishops' translation of Isaiah 5:14, "Therefore gapeth hell, and open her mouth marueilous wide," more closely than Geneva's "Hel hath inlarged itself."

What, however, does this tell us (at least about Shakespeare) beyond the fact that he was familiar with the English Bible in various versions? Was he recalling verses he had at some point heard in church, or had read on some occasion, or had picked up in conversation? It doesn't tell us which version, if any, he preferred, or why he preferred it. It would be convenient, for example, if we could show that his dependence on the Geneva translation dates from his time with the Mountjoys in London, but Geneva readings appear in plays written well before 1602 or 1603, when he had moved into the house of the Huguenot immigrants on Silver Street in Cripplegate.[69] But even if we could show that his familiarity with the Geneva translation[70] reflects his involvement with the Huguenot community, we can't know what he thought of the translation or what it meant for him. Perhaps he did find it theologically or ideologically compelling, or perhaps he merely found it close at hand. I don't know. No one does.

Ultimately, however, it seems to me not to matter very much whether or not Shakespeare owned a Geneva Bible or shared its theological commitments—or at least not to matter in the ways it has come to matter. It might matter if the plays could be explained by knowing what Shakespeare believed, but if that would explain them they would be much less interesting plays than in fact they are. And if they can't be explained by knowing what Shakespeare believed, then his faith should be important only as one more biographical fact—interesting in itself, as is the evidence of his real estate transactions, but of no great consequence in exploring how and why Shakespeare is actually significant to us.

But we want it to be. Shakespeare's religious belief seems like it might offer a clue to his artistic achievement in ways that his financial activities don't—or we think shouldn't. Perhaps this accounts for the fact that Malone never published his discovery of the undelivered letter Richard Quiney addressed to Shakespeare in 1598 requesting a loan of £30.[71] Religion seems fundamental. But we have better records of his finances than of his faith, and even this evidence of his worldliness comes to seem precious.

Who Shakespeare was does matter to many people, and the easy rejection of biography ("but, after all, it is the plays that matter") is belied by the passion with which that biography is sought and asserted, and by the enthusiasm with which we mine the writings for personal information. He is the writer who has survived the oft-published obituary that post-structuralism wrote for the author. We want to understand the mystery of his genius, know him as "the figure who is outside and precedes" what we read.[72] The ongoing search for an aristocratic Shakespeare (that is, a Shakespeare who is not Shakespeare) is motivated mainly by the belief that the glover's son from the Midlands market town was incapable of writing the works attributed to him. But, also, we often want to find Shakespeare to claim him—and the cultural capital he carries—as one of us, however "us" is intended, though often there is more at stake than the mere reflected glory of our affiliation. A Catholic Shakespeare (that is, a Shakespeare who could in fact be Shakespeare) would, for example, not merely allow some to claim Shakespeare as a co-religionist but also force a reconsideration of his role in the Protestant triumphalism that has for so long largely determined what Englishness is and has meant.

Yet if much may be at stake, little is certain—little, that is, beyond the fact that we want to believe in a Shakespeare who believed, as we once wanted a Shakespeare who was above all that. We now want to restore to him an interiority that has been…well, what? Buried? Concealed? Obscured? But isn't that somehow what interiority is? The part of us that is buried, concealed, obscured. To say (as I think) that Shakespeare's faith is undiscoverable is perhaps little more than a truism.

Or it might be thought an anachronism. The truism, it could be argued, is historically constructed and constrained; that it is only we (we moderns) who conceive of faith as inaccessible (and probably none of our business), the result of a process of secularization, still incomplete in Shakespeare's time, that privatized religion. I think, however, I'll stick to the truism. At the very least, the process of privatization was recognized, even encouraged, by an official policy that pragmatically declined to "make windows into men's hearts and secret thoughts,"[73] acknowledging that faith exists in a sphere of subjectivity into which neither Church nor Crown should peer, if indeed either could.

Inner lives are inner lives. They are not on display, and it is not only a modern squeamishness that prevents us from inquiring into them. Aesop's story of Momus criticizing the works of the gods circulated widely in early modern England, especially his critique of Jupiter's creation of man which, in Robert Greene's version in 1583, is said to be imperfect since the god "framed not a window in his brest, through which to perceiue his inward thoughts."[74]

The God of Genesis similarly framed no such window. "Inward thoughts" are inaccessible to others, a fact that the Elizabethan Settlement depended upon, contenting itself with enforcing only an outward conformity, even if, as many have observed, it thus settled too little and ensured that religion in the period was neither the *via media* that Elizabeth imagined nor the "constrained union" of papists and Protestants to which some of both objected.[75] Faith may be "the evidence of things not seen" (Hebrews 11.1), but it is itself something invisible, especially the faith of someone who died almost 400 years ago—and for whom, it must be admitted, there might have been prudent reasons to be circumspect about some of its contents. We can evaluate the sketchy evidence, reading it as responsibly and robustly as we can, trying to recover Shakespeare's faith from outer manifestations. But that formulation already presumes a relationship that is in doubt. It is mainly our will to believe certain things about Shakespeare (even, on occasion, that he was someone else) that we discover in the process. About his belief we must be, one might say, agnostic.

If I were forced to put a label on what I take to be Shakespeare's religious commitments—and I suppose it is far too late now to say that I don't care—I would say that he was probably something like what Christopher Haigh has termed a "Parish Anglican," a tolerant, largely habitual Christian, who recognized the "communal values of village harmony and worship and objected to the divisiveness of the godly."[76] Perhaps this marks him as Protestant in name only, but that was true of so many early modern English Christians, even many Catholics. Haigh at least provides a plausible, if slightly anachronistic, name for what I see in the plays: an inclusive and theologically minimalist Christianity that resisted religious rigor and valued social accord.[77] I like the term, though more on the grounds of its social identification than its confessional one. In emphasizing the "parish" rather than the church (which another suggested identification, "church papist,"[78] does emphasize even as it privatizes the actual matter of faith), "parish Anglican" gives voice to a wider frame of social engagement, which seems to me characteristic of Shakespeare, and indeed more so than any sectarian commitment. He seems to me at once too skeptical and too sympathetic to be zealously committed to any confession.

We are unable to pluck out the heart of his mystery from the historical record or from the body of work he has left us; nonetheless the effort to do so turns out to be useful, even if it must fail at the level of biography. What is valuable about the focus on Shakespeare's religion is not the non-confirmable conjectures about his belief. The plays' sensitive registers of and reflections upon the ways in which religious language, beliefs, practices, and ideas interact, forming and sometimes deforming individuals as well as the worlds they inhabit, are always in excess of not only what we can know about what Shakespeare believed but also for what that belief could be responsible. Focus on Shakespeare's religion gets the critical priorities backward, seeking in his faith both the impetus for and the significance of the complex dramatic exploration that the plays undertake, privileging the man over his writing, biography over art. Sometimes it is held that to misread the man is to misread the work, but our ability to "read" the man depends almost entirely upon our reading of the work, so the claim is meaningless.

Keats famously said that "Shakespeare led a life of Allegory: his works are the comments on it."[79] But an allegory of what? And Keats doesn't say that the works are the allegory of Shakespeare's life, which so many critics have wanted them to be. But allegory seems to me exactly what they are not, what they consciously refuse. Othello looks down at Iago's feet, thinking he must see the devil's cloven hooves, eager to allegorize his agonizing experience and, thus, evade the knowledge of his own partial responsibility for it. For Shakespeare, however, the "mystery of iniquity" rests in the human heart, and Othello immediately looks up, admitting: "but that's a fable" (5.2.283).

In one sense, it is obvious, as Northrop Frye said a long time ago, that "all commentary is allegorical interpretation."[80] Our acts of selecting and organizing our responses to a work produce meanings that are something other than a tautological reproduction of what we have read. But, in a more rigorous generic sense, responding to something as allegory assumes that what we have read, however imaginatively concentrated, is designed to prompt an engagement with ideas that exist somewhere other than in the ordering of the text; that it means, as Quintilian said, "one thing in the words, another in the sense."[81] A godly minister in 1617, writing on the Book of Revelation, reveals the same understanding: "as it is composed of such similitudes, so the words are figurative, the whole prophecie full of Metaphors, and almost altogether Allegoricall; so as we must take heede, that we looke further then into the letter and naked relation of things, as they are set downe."[82]

Derived from the Greek "*allos*" ("other") and "*agoreuo*" ("to speak publicly"), "allegory" is a form of displacement, using what is said overtly to point to its essential meanings, which the text, like some translucent veil, obscures but simultaneously calls attention to, creating the necessity for a disjunctive reading. Reading Shakespeare's plays *as* religious drama (except in a very weak sense that, in its generality, means basically that they are not) inevitably presumes this disjunction, often producing readings that seem to prove only that any text can be allegorized rather than that these texts should be. *The Comedy of Errors* may become a dramatic typology of English Catholicism, in which Luciana becomes "the patient, passively resistant new Catholicism of Shakespeare's own day," while her sister Adriana "represents old Catholicism, whose slackness drove the country into the arms of the reformers."[83] *Macbeth* can be read not as the story of a bloody struggle for the Scottish crown but as the figurative history of the English Reformation as a criminal imposition from above, with Macbeth and Lady Macbeth standing in for Henry VIII and Queen Elizabeth.[84] *King Lear* might be said "to present the predicament of a captive community, confined by penal laws to the desperate remedies of an inner exile, such as Edgar's disguise."[85]

It is largely those who argue for Shakespeare's Catholic sympathies who engage in such allegorization, usually on the grounds that the proscribed nature of the traditional faith demanded that sympathy for it be artfully hidden. But even when the religious meanings are less sectarian, the readings may seem no more persuasive. To one critic, Falstaff's conscription of Moldy, Shadow, Feeble, and Wart in *2 Henry IV* "suggests more than anything else Gideon's selection of a band to serve the Lord."[86] (More than *anything?*) And, more recently, another, in thinking about the nurse in *Romeo and Juliet* dating the weaning of Juliet by remembering an "earthquake now eleven years" (1.3.25), portentously reminds us that "[t]here was an earthquake too when Christ was thirsty on the cross. He was given 'gall,' and like Juliet 'when he had tasted thereof, he would not drinke' (Matt. 27:34)."[87]

What interests me in these examples is not (or at least not only) the implausibility of the particular reading but (also) what seems to me the category error that produces them. Shakespeare's plays do not seem to me "almost altogether Allegoricall" or even partially so. These readings seem to me to misconstrue both the genre of the works and how they relate to history or to revelation. Richard II does imagine himself as the betrayed Jesus delivered to his "sour cross" (4.1.241), but he is not a Christ figure except in his own self-pitying imagination. And that seems to me to be the point: the reference is designed to reveal something about Richard's psychology, not to serve as a pointer to an unwritten sacred history understood as more urgent and more essential than the world of human deeds and desires.

Shakespeare's religious belief is not the master narrative that either motivates or explains the plays, though the inescapable master narrative of Christianity itself in early modern England is always available to inflect (or deflect?) their meanings. His awareness of how religion shapes culture is everywhere evident. "If it is not plausible to read Shakespeare's play as Christian allegories," Debora Shuger sensibly argues, "neither is it likely that the popular drama of a religiously saturated culture could, by a secular miracle, have extricated itself from the theocentric orientation" of the age.[88] But religion in the plays doesn't so much answer our questions as provoke them, and Shakespeare's own faith cannot be discovered lurking provocatively behind what Graham Greene called his "smooth and ambiguous" writing.[89]

For some this elusiveness has become the very proof of Shakespeare's fugitive Catholicism,[90] the stylistic requirement of a faith that dares not speak its name, though, of course, it might as well be evidence of a more general circumspection about matters of religion, Catholic or otherwise, evidence of a reticence, or an impartiality, or even a geniality that seems more temperamental than tactical. "Gentle," after all, was the adjective the more contentious Ben Jonson at least twice applied to him, and it seems to be at least as much a comment on Shakespeare's disposition as on his social status.[91]

But the point is, unless one is willing to take its very inaccessibility as affirmative evidence for his belief, the nature of Shakespeare's faith, even its existence, remains unavailable to us. The religion of the plays can be confidently said to belong only to the fictional worlds rather than to their creator, but in the absence of an archive of biographical evidence, we make the work an allegory to fill in what we wish we had. How he experienced any of this personally we don't know, however much we want to. He remains for us, as Thomas Hardy called him, a "Bright baffling Soul...Leaving no intimate word or personal trace/Of high design outside the artistry/Of [his] penned dreams."[92]

Notes

1 *Selected Letters of John Keats*, ed. Grant F. Scott (Cambridge, MA and London: Harvard University Press, 2002), 60.

2 [Christopher Knight Watson], "Was Shakspeare [*sic*] a Roman Catholic," *The Edinburgh Review* 123 (1866), 184–5.

3 Carlyle, "Goethe," in *German Romance: Specimens of its Chief Authors* (Edinburgh: W. Tait, 1827), vol. 4, 22.

4 See, for example, Richard Wilson, *Secret Shakespeare: Studies in Theatre, Religion, and Resistance* (Manchester: Manchester University Press, 2004); Peter Milward, *Shakespeare the Papist* (Ann Arbor, MI: Sapientia Press, 2005); David N. Beauregard, *Catholic Theology in Shakespeare's Plays* (Newark, DE: University of Delaware Press, 2008); and, in a more popular mode, see Claire Asquith, *Shadowplay: The Hidden Beliefs and Coded Politics of William Shakespeare* (London: Perseus, 2005); Michael Wood, *In Search of Shakespeare* (London: BBC Books, 2007), to accompany the BBC television series; and Joseph Pearce, *The Quest for Shakespeare: The Bard of Avon and the Church of Rome* (San Francisco, CA: Ignatius Press, 2008).

5 John Stow, *Survey of London*, ed. C. L. Kingsford (Oxford: Clarendon Press, 1908), vol. 2, 75.

6 Taylor, "Forms of Opposition: Shakespeare and Middleton," *ELR* 24 (1994), 298; and Earle, *Micro-cosmographie* (London, 1628), sig. B7ᵛ. J. O. Halliwell-Phillipps had claimed that Shakespeare was "an outward conformist to the Protestant faith, but secretly attached to the old religion," *Outlines of a Life of Shakespeare* (New York: Longman, 1907), vol. 2, 428.

7 Greenblatt, *Hamlet in Purgatory* (Princeton, NJ: Princeton University Press, 2001), 249.

8 Eamon Duffy, *Saints, Sacrilege and Sedition: Religion and Conflict in the Tudor Reformation* (London: Bloomsbury, 2012), 234–46. It is certainly worth noting that both Duffy and Patrick Collinson have come down cautiously on the side of Shakespeare's traditionalism: Duffy says Shakespeare at the very least "must have struck alert contemporaries as a most unsatisfactory Protestant" (p. 253); and Collinson, in a discussion of recusancy, says of Shakespeare that "he may well have leaned in that direction," in his "William Shakespeare's Religious Inheritance and Environment," in *Elizabethan Essays* (London and Rio Grande, OH: Hambledon Press, 1994), 251.

9 In the Geneva version, the relevant section of Matthew 23:37 reads: "how often would I haue gathered thy children together, as yᵉ henne gathereth her chickens vnder her wings, and ye would not?"

10 Ireland, *Miscellaneous Papers and Legal Instruments Under the Hand and Seal of William Shakespeare* (London, 1796 [for 1795]), sig. A4ᵛ–A5ʳ.

11 Eamon Duffy seems to have invented the term "traditional religion" to recognize the resilience of post-Reformation Catholicism, which the phrase "old faith" might be thought to misrepresent and undervalue. See his *Stripping of the Altars: Traditional Religion in England c.1400–c.1580* (New Haven, CT and London: Yale University Press, 1992).

12 His will was witnessed by several neighbors, along with "Sir Wylliam Borton, curett," who in 1561 would be removed from the vicarship he then held for refusing the oath of supremacy. See Marc Eccles, *Shakespeare in Warwickshire* (Madison, WI: University of Wisconsin Press, 1961), 17–18.

13 On the Somerville Plot, and its relation to Shakespeare, see John D. Cox, "Local References in *3 Henry VI*," *Shakespeare Quarterly* 51 (2000), 340–52.

14 Samuel Schoenbaum, in his *William Shakespeare: A Documentary Life* (New York: Oxford University Press in association with Scolar Press, 1975), notes that the College of Heralds, in their consideration of the request to grant John Shakespeare a coat of arms, first designed a sketch including the arms of the Ardens of Park Hall, which they then scratched out, replacing it with a "less illustrious old coat," but in the end no Arden coat appeared on the Shakespeare shield (p.171). There is no indication of why the changes were made, though it is certainly possible that the Heralds ultimately rejected the idea that Mary, John Shakespeare's wife, was closely enough related to the Park Hall Ardens to merit the inclusion.

15 See Edgar I. Fripp, *Shakespeare Studies, Biographical and Literary* (Oxford: Oxford University Press, 1930), 84. In this period, the gentry of almost any English county, as Keith Wrightson reminds me, provides multiple examples of families with both Catholic and even radical Protestant members; e.g. the Winthrops, Suffolk Puritans, and prominent in the Massachusetts Bay Settlement, had a converted Catholic cousin with whom perfectly cordial relations were maintained.

16 Latimer, *Sermons and Remains of Hugh Latimer*, ed. George Elwis Corrie (Cambridge: Cambridge University Press, 1845), 384.

17 *The Book of Common Prayer: The Texts of 1549, 1559, and 1662*, ed. Brian Cummings (Oxford: Oxford University Press, 2011), 141, 146.

18 See John Cox's sensitive analysis of the two family baptisms and general consideration of what we know about Shakespeare's faith and what relation any of this might have for a reading of the plays in his valuable review essay of ten books on Shakespeare and religion, "Was Shakespeare a Christian, and If So, What Kind of Christian Was He," *Christianity and Literature* 55 (2006), 539–66. On the baptisms, see in particular pp. 540, 550; see also Edgar I. Fripp, *Shakespeare Studies, Biographical and Literary* (Oxford: Oxford University Press, 1930), 18–19.

19 The service was designed for the new mothers to give thanks for the "safe delyveraunce" of the child, and concluded with a monetary gift for the clergyman: "The woman that commeth to give her thanckes must offer accustomed offeryngs." See *The Book of Common Prayer: The Texts of 1549, 1559, and 1662*, ed. Brian Cummings (Oxford and New York: Oxford University Press, 2011), 175–6. See also Judith Maltby, *Prayer Book and People in Early Stuart England* (Cambridge: Cambridge University

Press, 1998), 52–6. It is her comment (p. 53) about the public and private sacrament above.

20 Edgar I. Fripp, *Minutes and Account of the Corporation of Stratford-upon-Avon and Other Records, 1153–1620* (Oxford: Oxford University Press, 1929, vol. 2, 140. See also Glynn Parry's "The Context of John Shakespeare's 'Recusancy' Re-examined," *Shakespeare Yearbook* 16 (2007), 1–38.

21 Fripp, *Minutes and Account*, vol. 4, 59.

22 See Michael Hodgetts, "A Certificate of Warwickshire Recusants, 1592," in *Worcester Recusant* 5 (1965), 20–31; and 6 (1965), 7–20.

23 Quoted in Robert Bearman, "John Shakespeare: A Papist or Just Penniless?" *Shakespeare Quarterly* 56 (2004), 428–9.

24 Bearman, "John Shakespeare: A Papist or Just Penniless?", 429 (emphasis mine). See also Glynn Parry's "The Context of John Shakespeare's 'Recusancy' Re-examined," esp. 15–27. For a defense of the Catholic recusant argument, see F. W. Brownlow, "John Shakespeare's Recusancy: New Light on an Old Document," *Shakespeare Quarterly* 40 (1989), 186–91.

25 Parry, 19–21.

26 Henry Sebastian Bowden, *The Religion of Shakespeare: Chiefly from the Writings of the Late Mr. Richard Simpson, M.A.* (London: Burns & Oates, 1899), 81. Peter Milward more cautiously claims the excuse "was a not uncommon subterfuge," in his *Shakespeare's Religious Background* (Bloomington, IN and London: Indiana University Press, 1973), 19.

27 It can be found as BRL 2510, 56–60.

28 *William Shakespeare, Plays and Poems*, ed. Edmond Malone (London, 1790), vol. 1, pt. 2, 162–6, 330–1.

29 See, for example, Halliwell-Phillips's certainty: "there can be no doubt that the whole of the paper is a modern fabrication," in *Outlines* (1907), vol. 2, 399; for a thorough if skeptical recent treatment, see Bearman, "John Shakespeare's 'Spiritual Testament,'" *Shakespeare Survey* 56 (2003), 184–202.

30 Thurston, "A Controverted Shakespeare Document," *The Dublin Review* 173 (1923), 161–76.

31 A printed English version dated 1635 exists in a bound collection of Catholic texts in the library of St. Mary's College, Oscott, in Birmingham, which was published in the series *English Recusant Literature, 1558–1640*, eds. David McGregor Rogers and David Morrison Rogers as vol. 140 (Menston: Scolar, 1973). In 1966, the Folger acquired a devotional book that included a printed English version published in 1638; see James G. McManaway, "John Shakespeare's Spiritual Testament," *Shakespeare Quarterly* 18 (1967), 197–205. These are the only two known English examples of the Testament other than the single manuscript version claimed to have been found in the Henley Street house.

32 Interestingly, Ireland had meet John Jordan in 1793 when he and his father visited Stratford; Jordan served as their guide. See *The Confessions of William-Henry Ireland* (London: Ellerton and Byworth, 1805), 19–26.

33 Malone wrote that "its contents are such as no one could have thought
    of inventing with a view to literary imposition." See "An Historical
    Account of the Rise and Progress of the English Stage," *William Shakespeare,
    Plays and Poems*, ed. Edmond Malone (London, 1790), vol. 1, pt. 2,
    162.

34 Bearman, "John Shakespeare's 'Spiritual Testament,'" 195.

35 See McManaway, "John Shakespeare's Spiritual Testament," *Shakespeare
    Quarterly* 18 (1967), 197–205. The testament as it was printed by Malone
    is reproduced in Schoenbaum, *William Shakespeare: A Documentary Life*,
    41–3.

36 Cf. "Cut off even in the blossoms of my sin," *Hamlet*, 1.5.76.

37 Malone, "An Historical Account of the Rise and Progress of the English
    Stage," *William Shakespeare, Plays and Poems*, vol. 1, pt. 2, 161.

38 Malone, *An Inquiry into the Authenticity of Certain Miscellaneous Papers*
    (London, 1796), 198–9.

39 *The Plays and Poems of William Shakespeare*, eds. Edmond Malone and
    James Boswell (London: 1821), vol. 2, 517, fn. 2.

40 Quoted in Peter Milward, *Shakespeare's Religious Background* (Bloomington,
    IN and London: Indiana University Press, 1973), 21.

41 Though, of course, it may be because very few, if any, reached England.
    It is often claimed that, as Patrick Collinson has said, English Jesuits
    requested "thousands of copies of this little classic of Counter-Reformation
    piety to distribute in England," but the evidence for this rests on letters
    speaking about "testaments" that seem more likely to refer to the Rheims
    New Testament rather than Borromeo's pamphlet-sized declaration of
    faith. See Patrick Collinson, "William Shakespeare's Religious Inherit-
    ance," in his *Elizabethan Essays*, p. 250; but see also Robert Bearman, "John
    Shakespeare's 'Spiritual Testament'", 192–5; and Thomas M. McCoog,
    S. J., and Peter Davidson, "Edmund Campion and William Shakespeare:
    Much Ado About Nothing," *The Reckoned Expense: Edmund Campion and the Early
    English Jesuits*, ed. Thomas M. McCoog, S. J., 2nd edn. (Rome: *Institutum
    Historicum Societatis Iesu*, 2007), 165–86.

42 Walsham, *Church Papists: Catholicism, Conformity and Confessional Polemic in
    Early Modern England* (London: The Royal Historical Society, 1993), 26.

43 Account book, 10 January 1563/4; reproduced in Fripp, *Shakespeare
    Studies, Biographical and Literary*, unnumbered page after p. 84.

44 Honan, *Shakespeare: A Life* (New York and Oxford: Oxford University
    Press, 1998), 15.

45 The absence of Shakespeare's name from the communion token books of
    St Saviour's Southwark has been taken by some, e.g. Eamon Duffy, "Was
    Shakespeare a Catholic," in *The Tablet* (27 April 1996), 537, as evidence
    of his non-conformity, but apparently only the names of heads of house-
    holds were recorded; see Jeremy Boulton, "The Limits of Formal Reli-
    gion: The Administration of Holy Communion in Late Elizabethan and
    Early Stuart England," *The London Journal* 102 (1984), 130–54.

46 Davies's additions to William Fullman's brief biographical note on Shakespeare are reproduced and transcribed in E. K. Chambers, *William Shakespeare: A Study of Facts and Problems* (Oxford: Clarendon Press, 1930), vol. 2, 257.

47 Richard Wilson, *Secret Shakespeare*, 56. See also E. K. Chambers, *The Elizabethan Stage* (Oxford: Clarendon Press, 1923), vol. 1, 280, on the Hoghton household and its possible connection to Shakespeare. See also Douglas Hamer, "Was William Shakespeare William Shakeshafte?" *Review of English Studies* 21 (1980), 41–8; Ernst Honigmann, *Shakespeare: The "Lost Years"* (Manchester: Manchester University Press, 1985), esp. 8–31; and Robert Bearman, "Was William Shakespeare William Shakeshafte Revisited," *Shakespeare Quarterly* 53 (2001), 83–94. Bearman reprints Hoghton's will from *Lancashire and Cheshire Wills and Inventories from the Ecclesiastical Court, Chester: The Second Portion*, ed. G. J. Piccope (Chetham Society, 1860), 237–41.

48 Schoenbaum, *William Shakespeare: A Documentary Life*, 243.

49 See J. D. Alsop, "Religious Preambles in Early Modern English Wills as Formulae," *Journal of Ecclesiastical History*, 40 (1989), 19–27, and Margaret Spufford, *Contrasting Communities: English Villagers in the Sixteenth and Seventeenth Centuries* (Cambridge: Cambridge University Press, 1974), 28–43.

50 Quoted in Duffy, *Stripping of the Altars*, 507.

51 Marsh, *Popular Religion in Sixteenth-Century England* (Basingstoke: Macmillan, 1998), 131.

52 William West, *The First Part of Simboleographie* (1605; London, 1615), sig. Oo7^v.

53 For an interesting account of what is decidedly unconventional in the will, see E. A. J. Honigmann, "Shakespeare on His Deathbed: The Last Will and Testament," in *Myriad-Minded Shakespeare: Essays on the Tragedies, Problem Comedies and Shakespeare the Man* (Basingstoke: Macmillan, 1989), 222–33.

54 In *English Playhouse Wills, 1558–1664*, eds. E. A. J. Honigmann and Susan Brock (Manchester and New York: Manchester University Press, 1993), 165, 156.

55 See Mark Eccles, *Shakespeare in Warwickshire* (Madison, WI: University of Wisconsin Press, 1961), 29–30.

56 Huggard, *The Displaying of the Protestantes* (London, 1556), sig. O5^v–O6^r.

57 Peter Lake, "Religious Identities in Shakespeare's England," in *A Companion to Shakespeare*, ed. David Scott Kastan (Oxford: Blackwell, 1999), 57–84.

58 Shapiro, *A Year in the Life of William Shakespeare: 1599* (New York: HarperCollins, 2005), 148.

59 See James Shapiro, *Contested Will: Who Wrote Shakespeare?* (New York: Simon and Schuster, 2010), 39–47 and *passim*, for a wonderful account of the problem of trying to read Shakespeare's biography out of his writing. Margreta DeGrazia, in her *Shakespeare Verbatim: The Representation*

of Authenticity and the 1790 Apparatus (Oxford: Clarendon Press, 1991), first recognized that it was Malone who was responsible for this, as he, in the frustrating absence of facts that would fully reveal the biographical Shakespeare, turned to the plays and poems for evidence: Shakespeare, "who had formally been distinguished for his accurate observation of others," was now cast "as the subject of his own writing, reflecting on his own psychological condition" (p. 159).

60 Wordsworth, "Scorn not the Sonnet."

61 Malone, *Supplement to the Edition of Shakespeare's Plays Published in 1778 by Samuel Johnson and George Steevens* (London, 1780), 653.

62 John Cox makes the important point that compared with Shakespeare, for whom "biblical allusions" were "ubiquitous," Montaigne "would choose Horace every time, given a choice between Horace and the gospels." See his *Seeming Knowledge: Shakespeare and Skeptical Faith* (Waco, TX: Baylor University Press, 2007), 29, 228–38.

63 See Richmond Noble, *Shakespeare's Biblical Knowledge and Use of the Book of Common Prayer* (London: Society for Promoting Christian Knowledge, 1935), and Naseeb Shaheen, *Biblical References in Shakespeare's Plays* (Newark, DE: University of Delaware Press, 1999).

64 Article VI, "The Thirty-Nine Articles of Religion," *Book of Common Prayer*, ed. Cummings, 675.

65 *Book of Common Prayer*, 750.

66 On the history of the translation of the Bible into English in the sixteenth century, see David Daniell, *The Bible in English: Its History and Influence* (New Haven, CT: Yale University Press, 2003); S. L. Greenslade, "English Versions of the Bible," in *The Cambridge History of the Bible, Vol. 3: The West from the Reformation to the Present Day* (Cambridge: Cambridge University Press, 1963), 141–74; and David Norton, *A History of the English Bible as Literature* (Cambridge: Cambridge University Press, 2000).

67 Norton, *A History of the English Bible as Literature*, 104.

68 Although "narrow gate" does appear in the Rheims translation and not in the earlier Protestant translations, it is nonetheless common to see it in the writings of obviously Protestant writers. "Narrow gate," for example, appears in Arthur Dent's enormously popular *Sermon on Repentence*, where he urges the faithful to "striue to enter in at the narrow gate" (1582, sig. C8ʳ), and even Miles Coverdale in his *Fruitfull Lessons* refers to the "narrowe gate that wee must enter in at" (1593, sig. Aa3ᵛ). Shakespeare, thus, could have easily picked it up without access to Rheims. But this merely demonstrates my general point that biblical language gets paraphrased and pulled from various translations by Shakespeare and other writers without necessarily suggesting confessional allegiance.

69 Charles Nicholl, *The Lodger: Shakespeare on Silver Street* (London: Allen Lane, 2007); see also John W. Velz, "Shakespeare and the Geneva Bible: The Circumstances," *Shakespeare, Marlowe, and Jonson: New Directions in Biography,*

eds. Takashi Kozuka and J. R. Mulryne (Aldershot: Ashgate, 2006), 113–18. Velz makes the connection with the Mountjoys, but also suggests that Shakespeare's entry into the Huguenot community may have come earlier through Richard Field's wife, Jacqueline, the widow of the Huguenot printer, Thomas Vautrollier, to whom Field had been apprenticed.

70 Shaheen, *Biblical References in Shakespeare's Plays*, 48: "Shakespeare was best acquainted with the Geneva Bible and the Psalter."

71 Malone apparently discovered the document in 1793, but it was not published until Boswell included it in the 1821 *Variorum*. See Schoenbaum, *William Shakespeare: A Documentary Life*, 180.

72 Michel Foucault, "What is an Author?" *Language, Counter-Memory, Practice: Selected Essays and Interviews*, ed. Donald F. Bouchard (Ithaca, NY: Cornell University Press, 1977), 115.

73 The phrase is Bacon's; see "Certain Observations Made upon a Libel Published in this Present Year, 1592," in *The Works of Francis Bacon*, eds. James Spedding, Robert Leslie Ellis, and Douglas Denon Heath (London: Longman, Green, Longman, and Roberts, 1862), vol. 8, 178.

74 Greene, *Mamillia: A Mirrour or Looking-Glasse for the Ladies of Englande* (London, 1583), sig. G3ᵛ.

75 See, among many fine studies considering the Elizabethan Settlement, William P. Haugaard, *Elizabeth and The English Reformation: The Struggle for a Stable Settlement of Religion* (Cambridge: Cambridge University Press, 1968); Patrick Collinson, *The Religion of Protestants: The Church in English Society 1559–1625* (Oxford: Clarendon Press, 1982); Judith Maltby, *Prayer Book and People in Elizabethan and Early Stuart England* (Cambridge: Cambridge University Press, 1998); Diarmaid MacCulloch, *The Later Reformation in England, 1547–1603*, rev. edn. (Basingstoke: Macmillan, 2000); Norman L. Jones, *The English Reformation: Religion and Cultural Adaptation* (Oxford: Blackwell, 2002); and Eamon Duffy, *Saints, Sacrilege and Sedition*.

76 Christopher Haigh, *English Reformations: Religion, Politics, and Society under the Tudors* (Oxford: Clarendon, Press, 1993), 291.

77 This is a view of a Shakespeare not all that different, except in the level of religious commitment, from the irenic and "accommodationist" Shakespeare that Jeffrey Knapp describes in *Shakespeare's Tribe*, 49–54; and/or the undogmatic and philosophically skeptical Shakespeare that John D. Cox sees in his *Seeming Knowledge: Shakespeare and Skeptical Faith*, 1–29.

78 Taylor, "Forms of Opposition: Shakespeare and Middleton," *English Literary Renaissance* 24 (1994), 298.

79 *Selected Letters of John Keats*, 261.

80 Frye, *Anatomy of Criticism* (Princeton, NJ: Princeton University Press, 1957), 89.

81 Quintilian, *Institutio Oratio*, trans. H. E. Butler (Cambridge, MA: Harvard University Press, 1921), 8.6.44. The original reads "*aliud verbis aliud sensu.*"

82 Richard Bernard, *A Key of Knowledge for the Opening of the Secret Mysteries of St. John's Mysticall Revelation* (London, 1617), sig. N1ᵛ. Bernard, interestingly, here turns to a theatrical metaphor for the Revelation, which he says offers an image of the whole "Comicall tragedy, or tragicall Comedie that was...to be acted vpon the stage of this world."

83 Claire Asquith, *Shadowplay*, 59.

84 Peter Milward finds the "main theme" of *Macbeth* in its parallels with the early history of the Reformation in England. Macbeth's murderous acts that allow him to achieve and maintain the Scottish crown recall Henry VIII's "unheard of usurpation" in claiming supreme headship over the Church of England, "followed up by the execution of all who refused to accept it, even those like Sir Thomas More who persisted in silence." See his *Catholicism of Shakespeare's Plays* (Southampton: Saint Austin Press, 1997), 63.

85 Wilson, *Secret Shakespeare*, 283.

86 J. A. Bryant, Jr., "Prince Hal and the Ephesians," *Sewanee Review* 67 (1959), 218.

87 Beatrice Groves, *Texts and Traditions: Religion in Shakespeare 1592–1604* (Oxford and New York: Oxford University Press, 2007), 63.

88 Shuger, "Subversive Fathers and Suffering Subjects: Shakespeare and Christianity," in *Religion, Literature, and Politics in Post-Reformation England, 1540–1688*, eds. Donna B. Hamilton and Richard Strier (Cambridge: Cambridge University Press, 1996), 46.

89 Greene, "Introduction," *John Gerard: The Autobiography of an Elizabethan*, ed. and trans. Philip Caraman (London: Longmans, 1951), x–xi.

90 See, among others, Richard Wilson, *Secret Shakespeare*, 165 and *passim*.

91 Twice in the 1623 Folio Jonson refers to him as "gentle Shakespeare": in his prefatory poem "To the Reader" and in his "To the memory of my beloued, The Avthor Mr. William Shakespeare: And what he hath left vs."

92 Hardy, "To Shakespeare: After Three Hundred Years," in *Complete Poems of Thomas Hardy*, ed. James Gibson (London, Macmillan, 1984), 370.

3

All Roads Lead to Rome

The absence of dogma, which is one of the most conspicuous
and highly valued aspects of Shakespeare's writings, militates
against the hypothesis that he adhered strongly to a doctrinaire
creed.

Stanley Wells

Sometimes it has seemed to be so: that all Shakespearean roads lead
us to Rome, to the possibility of Shakespeare's Catholicism. But if
they do, it has often depended, as I have already argued, upon a
willful reading of both the historical record and the literary remains.
What interests me here is not, however, the question of whether
Shakespeare was a Catholic, but a consideration of the presentation
of Catholics and Catholicism in the plays. It should be clear by now
that I don't think there is a way to know anything for sure about
what Shakespeare believed.

Nonetheless, whether or not Shakespeare believed as a Catholic or
grew up in a Catholic household, there can be little doubt that he
can no longer straightforwardly serve as the national poet of a godly
nation, as he did for so long.[1] Such a view could be maintained only
by knowingly obscuring too much of what we now understand about
both the poet and the nation. Spiritual, affective, and material
remains of the traditional religion mark both Shakespeare and his
England, not as some sticky residue that cannot quite be removed
but as something constitutive in the makeup of each. Whether the
Reformation was motivated from above or below, it was, in either
case, incomplete; and Shakespeare, although his own faith seems
indeterminable, unquestionably reveals an awareness of and perhaps
even a sympathy for much of what resisted the reform.

Critics have been assiduous in searching the plays for the evidence of his attraction to the traditional religion, finding it either conspicuously exhibited, and therefore indisputable evidence of his Catholic sympathies, or ingeniously concealed, and therefore also indisputable evidence of his Catholic sympathies. What, however, seems to me important, and largely unremarked, about his handling of Catholic elements is how often they neither display nor hide themselves. They don't seem to need to. They are just there. Catholic elements are matter-of-factly presented in many of the plays, in some cases, of course, merely as a result of the Italian setting, although this must raise the question of why he set so many plays in a Catholic country in the first place.

In the histories, of course, the presence of Catholic clergy is no less a function of the choice of setting, but one could not write *Richard III*, say, without setting it in pre-Reformation England. *Two Gentleman of Verona*, on the other hand, could as easily have been *Two Gentleman of Uttoxeter*. The plot does not require an Italian setting, and in this case not even the source stipulates it.[2] But Proteus offers to be Valentine's "beadsman," offering up "holy prayers" on his behalf (1.1.17–18), Sylvia intends "holy confession" at "Friar Patrick's cell" (4.3.43–4), "Friar Laurence" wanders through the forest doing "penance" (5.2.35–6), Julia sees herself as a "true-devoted pilgrim" (2.7.9) in following Proteus, and she takes the name of Sebastian, a Christian martyr, for her disguise.

The world of the play is marked as unmistakably Catholic, but what seems to me noteworthy is not that this is charged with meaning but that it isn't. The Catholic references here seem more a kind of Barthesian reality-effect than a provocative symbolic setting. They are more or less unmotivated, only barely functioning within the narrative or symbolic economies of the play.[3] They do not seem to register the fact that they could be (literally) controversial. Indeed, they seem more compelling as romance details than "Romanist" ones, establishing the genre rather than the theology of the play. Or maybe better, they establish a genre that demands the theology of the play—a required Catholicism that justifies notice only because nothing is made of it, or, even more exactly, because it is made into nothing. Friars are named but never appear on stage; there is a "brother...in the cloister" (1.3.2) but it is only Antonio's brother talking in an arbored walkway; Proteus is no "beadsman" but rather Valentine's wing-man, and his "prayers" for Valentine are hardly "holy"; Sylvia never gets to confess to Friar Patrick, and her pilgrimage is a rather worn metaphor for a love quest, neither elevated nor degraded by the religious language that serves only to indicate its emotional intensity.

I suppose one could find in this vanishing of the Catholic elements an allegory of Catholicism in early modern England, a kind of literary priest's hole where Catholicism hides to evade detection.[4] I don't believe that is the case, but at the very least Shakespeare refuses the stigmatization of the Italian romances that was common among hot Protestants, not on the predictable moral grounds on which they might be criticized as "the *Siren* songes of *Italie*," but on theological ones. Roger Ascham, for example, condemns the "fonde bookes of late translated out of *Italian* into English, sold in euery shop in London," which function "not so moch to corrupt honest liuyng, as they do to subuert trewe Religion.... Mo Papistes be made, by your mery bookes of *Italie*, than by your earnest bookes of *Louain*."[5] Shakespeare seems more sanguine: sometimes Italy is just Italy, and an Italian, just an Italian.

Usually, however, the Catholicism of the setting remains more visible than it does in *Two Gentleman*. Think of Shakespeare's other Verona play. In *Romeo and Juliet* Catholicism does not as easily disappear into metaphor or refuse its theatrical realization. It is unavoidable, more deeply woven into both the language and the action. It is clearly not mere local color, but neither is there any frisson of transgression. This play does not merely talk of friars but lets us see and hear them.

Friar Laurence is a "ghostly father" (2.3.45), but, unlike Hamlet's, he is clearly flesh and blood. "Ghostly" here, of course, means spiritual rather than spectral, and the role is the third largest in the play. Only the title characters speak more lines. The Friar is dressed and addressed in his holiness: Old Capulet calls him a "reverend holy friar" (4.2.31); to the nurse he is a "holy friar" (3.3.81). Juliet reassures herself that "he hath still been tried a holy man" (4.3.29). And, even at the end, when things have gone horrifyingly wrong in part because of the Friar's actions, the Prince reassures him that "[w]e still have known thee for a holy man" (5.3.270).

None of this is colored by irony. His holiness is confirmed by the verbal repetition, not undercut by it, as, say, Brutus's honor is by Antony's repetition of "honourable" in *Julius Caesar*. The Friar not only seeks to ensure that the lovers' passion leads to lawful marriage, but also works to repair Verona's frayed social bonds, hoping "this alliance may so happy prove/To turn your households' rancour to pure love" (2.3.91–2). Nonetheless, he is in some sense responsible for the tragedy and perhaps should be blamed most for ignoring his office, in Romeo's words, as "a divine, a ghostly confessor,/A sin absolver" (3.3.49–50). Where the Friar might have counseled shrift, instead he suggests deception, and the plot ultimately confirms his own intuition that "[c]onfusion's cure lies not/In these confusions" (4.5.65–6). But even this suggests the matter-of-factness with which the play's Catholicism affirms itself, even if the tragedy is at least in part a function of the Friar's failure to act as a friar, in ministering to Romeo's heart instead of his soul.

One could hold him to a strict account, not only for failing to shrive either Romeo or Juliet, but also in agreeing to perform a clandestine marriage, though both the Roman and the English Church forbade priests to perform such weddings, and in encouraging Juliet to lie to enable hers ("Go home, be merry, give consent/To marry Paris," 4.1.89–90). Arthur Brooke, in his preface to his *Tragicall Historye of Romeus and Iuliet*, the poem that served as the immediate source of Shakespeare's play, condemns the lovers for "vsyng auricular confession (the key of whoredome, and treason) for furtheraunce of theyr purpose, abusing the name of honorable marriage."[6] But in *Romeo and Juliet* it is not that the sacrament of penance is in any sense corrupt. Indeed it is precisely that it isn't, but that the sacrament hasn't been embraced. Unlike *The Tragicall Historye*, where Friar Laurence serves, at least in Brooke's polemical preface, as an example of "superstitious friers (the naturally fitte instrumentes of vnchastitie),"[7] Shakespeare's play presents him as well-meaning, though ineffective—and arguably ineffective in no small part because he rejects his proper priestly role.

In *Much Ado about Nothing*, which of course is also set in Italy—in Messina—we have another friar who is conspicuously present but who, unlike the Friar in *Romeo and Juliet*, performs his clerical role well. Significantly, this is a role that Shakespeare invents, not being part of the Bandello novella upon which the play is based. Friar Francis is in attendance to officiate at the wedding ceremony of Hero and Claudio, and when it is broken off by Claudio's brutal determination "Not to be married, not to knit my soul/To an approved wanton" (4.1.42–3), it is the Friar who correctly intuits her innocence: "trust not my age,/My reverence, calling nor divinity,/ If this sweet lady lie not guiltless here/Under some biting error" (4.1.167–170). With Hero generally thought to be dead, the Friar counsels to "Let her awhile be secretly kept in,/And publish it that she is dead indeed" (4.1.203–4). It is a less elaborate and therefore more reliable version of the plan of Friar Laurence in *Romeo and Juliet*; and, with the help of Dogberry and the watch, it allows the lovers a necessary second chance. The play ends with Friar Francis ready once again to celebrate the "holy rites" in "the chapel" (5.4.68, 71), marrying Hero and Claudio, while Benedick, that committed bachelor, also hopes "this day to be conjoined/In the estate of honourable marriage,/In which, good Friar, I shall desire your help" (5.4.29–31). Although the ceremonies are not seen performed, the promised comic end depends upon the Friar's conspicuous ministry.

In all the plays set in contemporary Italy, Shakespeare stages Catholicism without any of the hostility with which English Protestant polemic characteristically treated it. It is not presented as sinister or corrupt but as a religion that effectively serves the emotional and spiritual needs of the society of the play. Robert Greene writes of the "rascall Rable of the Romish Church, as Monkes, Friers, dirging Priestes...sitting banqueting with faire Nunnes, hauing store of Cates, and wines before them, stall-fed with ease and gluttony."[8] And when Mephistopheles first appears to Doctor Faustus in Marlowe's play, Faustus tells the demon to "change thy shape:/Thou art too ugly to attend on me./Go, and return an old Franciscan friar;/ That holy shape becomes a devil best" (1.3.25–6). But Shakespeare indulges in none of this familiar corrosive anti-fraternalism, which, it must be said, is not inevitably anti-Catholic. There is a long medieval history of it, best known perhaps in Boccaccio and Chaucer; but once Luther identifies "whoever serves this or that holy order, to him we give a sure promise of eternal life" as "sacrilegious words,"[9] it inevitably becomes so.

In Shakespeare's plays, however, friars cross the stage, presumably robed and sandaled, clearly identifiable, at least in *Romeo and Juliet*, as Franciscans, wholesomely engaged in pastoral activities like "visiting the sick" in a time of plague (5.2.7). They are neither demonic nor demonized. Their presence seems problematic only insofar as they fail in their clerical obligations, and is so natural in the plays that it is rarely if ever observed that their actions on stage would have been impossible in the streets of Shakespeare's England. Mendicant friars in England mostly disappeared after their houses were dissolved in 1538 and 1539,[10] but there was a continued anxiety about "Begging Friars sent abroad and emploied by the Romans, to set vpon those that dare open their mouthes against their Domination" (sig. G3ᵛ), as a chapter heading has it in the zealously titled, *A discouery of the great subtiltie and wonderful wisedome of the Italians whereby they beare sway ouer the most part of Christendome, and cunninglie behaue themselues to fetch the quintescence out of the peoples purses: discoursing at large the meanes, howe they prosecute and continue the same: and last of all, conuenient remedies to preuent all their pollicies herein* (London, 1591). Proclamations were issued warning against the presence of "friars, priests, Jesuits, or popish scholars," who, "under a false color and face of holiness [seek] to make breaches in men's and women's consciences and so to train them to their treason,"[11] and legislation was passed in 1585 ordering Catholic priests ordained since 1559 to leave England within forty days or be liable to the death penalty, a law reconfirmed in the first year of James's reign.[12]

That any of these plays were played, and had in the case of *Romeo and Juliet* enough success to be many "times publiquely acted," as well as to justify five published playbooks by 1637, indicates that no one in authority recognized anything threatening in them. There were repeated governmental decrees objecting to the fact that "the players take upon themselves to handle in their plaies certen matters of Divinytie and State, unfitt to be suffered," often explicitly prohibiting "anythinge plaied which tende to the maintenaunce of superstition and idolatrie."[13] But none of Shakespeare's Italian plays attracted any official attention.

Perhaps it was because Catholic sacramental practice is merely named rather than enacted (unlike, say, the episode in 1639, when actors at the Fortune Theatre were fined a draconian £1000 for "setting up an altar, a bason, and two candlesticks, and bowing down before it upon the stage"[14]). Or maybe because any polemical religious intent has the advantage of deniability, as the Catholic elements are narratively plausible as requisite aspects of the dramatic fiction. Or, possibly merely because the plays were set in Verona and Messina rather than in Rome, which might indeed have set off alarms (and in which, maybe significantly, Shakespeare set only pre-Christian classical plays). But, for whatever reason, these were played and printed without apparent concern from any official that their treatment of religion might be subversively designed to effect the reconciliation of the culture to an officially proscribed Catholicism, and until recently their treatment of Catholicism had passed virtually without comment. *Romeo and Juliet* was a play about teenage lovers trying—and failing—to make their way through the minefields of incompetent parents and urban violence, rather than a play in any fundamental sense about religious belief and practice.

It cannot be that this is evidence of Shakespeare's skillful disguise of his Catholic sympathies, because if the sympathies *are* Catholic they are not disguised. Perhaps, as in Poe's "Purloined Letter," they remain hidden from view precisely by being placed in plain sight. But it is simpler to think they are placed in plain sight because there was no need to hide them from view. These examples tell us nothing at all about Shakespeare's faith but something important about Shakespeare's England: that at least at certain moments Catholicism could be represented, especially at a distance, as something more or less neutral. It needn't be the bogey that it was in Protestant polemic. Its presence in these plays is evidence not only, as has become the new historical orthodoxy, of the inadequacy of a conception of English religion that refuses to admit the resilience of Catholic elements and commitments, but also, and more interestingly, of the inadequacy of a conception of English Protestantism that refuses to admit that there were alternatives to the strident anti-Catholicism by which it sometimes defined itself.

Peter Lake has brilliantly analyzed how Protestantism used a view of Catholicism as its mirror opposite to assert and consolidate "the integrity of a Protestant England,"[15] but Lake himself is well aware of how inadequate the almost Manichean view of their confessional antagonism is to describe the reality of much (or even most) of the daily experience of Protestant religious life in early modern England. Family and friendship networks regularly formed across confessional divides. King James complained in 1614 that recusancy laws were hard to enforce because officials "were kin or friends of the papists,"[16] and the Calvinist Joseph Hall lamented the ways in which Protestants intermingled with their Catholic neighbors: "We match, confer, consult with them carelessly."[17]

But inevitably that was the case. Protestant polemic would define Catholicism as a foreign and false religion, but for most English Protestants Catholicism was native and familiar—and even calling it false was troubling, for that must have raised disturbing questions about the souls of their parents and grandparents, who were likely to have died in the old faith.[18] For all its polemical power, the polarized model of confessional allegiance not only fails to define the reality of early modern English religious identity, but also its sharp polarization actually contributed to the contradictions and inconsistencies of religious practice that have been made apparent by historians like Peter Lake, Patrick Collinson, Christopher Haigh, Michael Questier, Ethan Shagan, Norman Jones, and Alexandra Walsham.[19] The more Protestant polemic demonized its Catholic other, as another of these historians, Anthony Milton, has said, "the more incongruous it would seem to apply this model to friends or neighbors (or, indeed, to the country's own past)."[20]

The very fact that religion in these plays drew no official rebuke or seemingly even scrutiny suggests, among other things, that sympathetic treatment of Catholicism was not inevitably a cultural red flag. If Italians were Catholic that was all right—at least as long as they stayed in their own country. Or maybe the disregard was because the Church in these plays is represented by compassionate mendicant priests rather than the higher clergy, who might be more dangerous, at least in part because they seem more easily to be corrupted by the lures of this world.

Catholics in England, however, were unquestionably more unsettling. In the history plays set in pre-Reformation England, the clergy of course are Catholic, but in these plays they are rarely the well-intentioned presences they are in the Italian plays. Perhaps the closest to the benign Italian friars is the priest who serves as young Rutland's tutor in *3 Henry VI*, on stage for just nine lines. As Clifford and his storm troopers come for the boy, the priest helplessly tries to protect him, warning Clifford against the murder of the innocent, even offering to die with his charge; but Clifford in his vengeful fury hardly notices him: "thy priesthood saves thy life" (1.3.3), he says dismissively, before ordering his soldiers to take him away. A benevolent and even a brave priest—but totally impotent.

Seemingly similar in motive if more effective is the archbishop in *Richard III*, who conducts the Queen and the young Duke of York to sanctuary at Westminster. But here he will finally defend neither the weak nor even the principle of sanctuary, quickly bowing to Buckingham's legalisms and delivering up the Prince to Buckingham and Richard. This is but a particular craven example of the behavior of the high clergy in the English histories. They are for the most part worldly creatures attracted to and wielding power, often using religion to mask and legitimate decidedly secular ambitions and desires. The Archbishop of York in *2 Henry IV* is praised by his fellow rebels for the success with which he "[t]urns insurrection to religion" (1.1.201), using his authority as a Churchman to draw support for the rebellion. In *1 Henry VI*, Gloucester correctly upbraids Henry Beaufort, then the Bishop of Winchester and soon to be cardinal, for his hypocrisy: "Name not religion, for thou lov'st the flesh,/And ne'er throughout the year to church thou goest—/Except it be to pray against thy foes" (1.1.41–3). But the attack in the histories is on the person, not the Church. "Thou art reverend/Touching thy spiritual function, not thy life," says Gloucester to Beaufort. When the bishop bridles at the insult, sputtering, "Rome shall remedy this," Gloucester puns sardonically: "Roam thither, then" (3.1.49–51).

Some roads, I guess, do lead to Rome, but only in *King John* is there an attack on the Church of Rome itself. John's reign might well be thought an odd choice of subject for Shakespeare, interrupting his sustained dramatic investigation of history from the deposition of Richard II to the coming of the Tudors (although, of course, these eight plays were not written in this order). King John had been rescued from the contempt the monastic historians had heaped upon him in large part by the efforts of John Bale. Sometime about 1537, probably on commission for Lord Cromwell's players,[21] Bale turned the inherited portrait of an incompetent and avaricious king into a proto-Protestant hero-martyr, who was willing to resist, if finally forced to submit to, a corrupt pope.

Though Bale's play is far more intellectually subtle than it is usually given credit for, its politics are blunt and not at all nuanced, as the morality play gets reformatted for contemporary concerns. The vice figure Sedition becomes the papal legate, Stephen Langton, who conspires with a monk to poison John; Private Wealth is Cardinal Pandulph; Usurped Power is the Pope; Treason enters as a priest. King Johan valiantly attempts to protect widow England from Catholic predation, and though he fails, the play looks to the eventual success of the Reformation as Imperial Majesty, clearly Henry VIII, assumes his proper role as "the supreme head of the Churche" (l. 2389) and "the true defender" (l. 2427) of the faith and the nation that embodies it.

Shakespeare's play, however, is no Protestant polemic. His John is deeply flawed, stripped of the heroic qualities with which Bale had endowed him. John is clearly a usurper and an opportunist. He has only a "borrowed majesty," and he is willing to suborn murder to preserve it. Nonetheless, the Catholic Church appears here as a scheming and predatory enemy, eager to undermine England's national sovereignty and to poison its king. John is certainly not Bale's proto-Protestant hero, but the Church here *is* arguably Bale's villain. Shakespeare takes the English king, who, with the exception of Henry VIII, is most closely identified with the break from Rome, and undoes the aura that sixteenth-century Protestant writers had provided for him. But he refuses merely to flip the valence of the story, declining to reinstate the medieval chroniclers' view of the history.

The frustrating ambivalence of Shakespeare's play would, in different historical circumstances, inspire Colley Cibber to adapt the play in 1736, hoping, as he later said, to "inspirit [Shakespeare's] King *John* with a resentment that might justly become an *English* monarch, and to paint the intoxicated tyranny of *Rome* in its proper colours," that is, hoping to turn Shakespeare's *King John* back into Bale's in response to the threat of a Jacobite uprising. Indeed Cibber, in his dedication of the play to the Earl of Chesterfield, wondered how to account for Shakespeare's seeming neutrality in "the flaming contest between his insolent *Holiness* and King John":

Shall we suppose, that in those days, almost in the infancy of the reformation, when Shakespeare wrote, when the influence of the papal power had a stronger party left than we have reason to believe is now subsisting among us; that this, I say, might make him cautious of offending? Or shall we go so far for an excuse, as to conclude that Shakespeare was himself a Catholic?[22]

In the event Cibber would refuse to go that far ("the conjecture is too strong" and the scene offers no "declaration of [Shakespeare's] own faith").[23] But the very title of Cibber's adaptation, *Papal Tyranny in the Reign of King John*, declares *his* own faith and the intentions that follow from it. Shakespeare, on the other hand, neatly balances John's moral failures against those of the Church. With young Arthur's death, "[t]he life, the right, and the truth of all this realm/Is fled to Heaven" (4.3.144–5), as the Bastard says, although Arthur's youth and foreign birth complicate his claim. But the play clearly does not find any more certain grounding either in John's compromised rule, which even his mother admits depends on "Your strong possession much more than your right" (1.1.40), or in the international ambitions of the Catholic Church, which undermine the Erastian claims of King John.

Pandolph, the Cardinal of Milan, comes "religiously to demand" (3.1.66) that John appoint Stephen Langton Archbishop of Canterbury, and John refuses. He defies the Pope's "usurped authority" (3.1.86; and remember Bale's typology), as English monarchs would come to do only with the Supremacy Act of 1534 (repealed under Mary and reinstated under Elizabeth), asserting that "as we, under God, are supreme head,/So under Him that great supremacy/Where we do reign, we will alone uphold/Without the assistance of a mortal hand./So tell the Pope" (3.1.81–5). The proud assertion of supremacy would have, for most in the audience, been heard with patriotic delight. "[No] Italian priest/Shall tithe or toll in our dominions" (3.1.79–80), says King John, and the play demands assent to the speech, if not to the speaker, reinforcing similar concerns about papal intervention and the activities of foreign priests that were being spoken by officials throughout the 1590s.

To the French king's shocked description of this as blasphemy, John replies proleptically with a familiar Protestant denunciation of the corruption and hypocrisy of the Catholic Church:

> Though you and all the kings of Christendom
> Are led so grossly by this meddling priest,
> Dreading the curse that money may buy out,
> And by the merit of vile gold, dross, dust,
> Purchase corrupted pardon of a man,
> Who, in that sale, sells pardon from himself;
> Though you and all the rest so grossly led
> This juggling witchcraft with revenue cherish,
> Yet I alone, alone do me oppose
> Against the Pope and count his friends my foes.
>
> (3.1.88–97)

John's proto-Protestant emphasis upon the economics of salvation ("money," "buy," "gold," "purchase," "sale," "revenue," etc.), and his assertion of an English exceptionalism ("I alone, alone do me oppose") draws the fury of the Cardinal, who pronounces John's excommunication, as Pope Paul III had done to Henry VIII on 17 December 1538 (renewing a suspended bull of 1535), and as Pius V had to Elizabeth on 27 April 1570:

> Then, by the lawful power I have,
> Thou shalt stand cursed and excommunicate,
> And blessed shall he be that doth revolt
> From his allegiance to an heretic;
> And meritorious shall that hand be called,
> Canonized and worshipped as a saint,
> That takes away by any secret course
> Thy hateful life.
>
> (3.1.98–105)

However audiences might have heard either John's or Pandolph's words, it is hard to see how they could be taken as evidence of Shakespeare's secret Catholicism or even of much lingering sympathy for it. Too clearly it plays to the same anti-Catholicism of so much English patriotic writing in the 1590s. There are ironies here, but not concerning the treatment of the Church of Rome. Perhaps the clearest evidence of the difficulty *King John* poses for the idea of a Catholic Shakespeare can be found in a copy of the 1632 Second Folio, now in the Folger Library in Washington DC,[24] but which had made its way into the library of St Alban's College, a Jesuit seminary established by Robert Persons in 1589 at Valladolid in Spain.

Sometime in the mid 1640s, a college official expurgated the volume. Although the first public mention in England of this censored Second Folio, in a note in *The Times* on 10 April 1922, was entitled "Shakespeare and the Inquisition," by the great Shakespearean Sidney Lee, the expurgated copy was not directly associated with the activity of the Inquisition. No works of Shakespeare ever appeared in any *Index of Prohibited Books*, in Spain or anywhere else, and yet, on the bottom of its title page is written in ink what is in effect a license: "*Opus auctoritate Sancti officij permissum et expurgatum eadum auctoritate per Guillielmum Sanchaeum e Soc.ᵗᵉ Jesu.*" This is not censorship but an allowance: the book in its expurgated form is certified as now fit to be read by the seminary students. One of the five written rules for the seminary's collection of books insisted that "Care is to be taken that there are no harmful or profane books in the library."[25] The expurgation is the mark of that "care," an act designed to ensure that the Shakespeare folio is neither "harmful" nor "profane," while the license on the title page attests that the work to achieve this has been, one might say, faithfully done.

Though the Folger catalogue identifies the licenser as Guillermo Sanchez, it is clear that this is, as Roland Frye had assumed, the work of the English Jesuit William Sankey, who was active at the college in Vallodolid by 1641 and then appointed rector of the English college in Madrid in 1651. Sankey often signed official documents with a Spanish version of his name, Guillermo Sanchez, or the Latin version, Gullielmus Sanchaeus.[26] Similar authorizations to that on the Second Folio appear on the title pages of other English books in the Vallodolid Library, as well as similar censorings of their pages, including a copy of John Speed's *Historie of Great Britain* (1631), which also shows signs of expurgations designed to make the book acceptable for the seminarians to read. In Speed's *Historie* "there are deletions in passages concerning the papacy during the reigns of King John, Henry III, Richard II. Pages 1025 to 1028 on Henry

VIII are entirely removed. A poem about the Armada is erased and pages 1229 to 1236 about the Gunpowder Plot are removed."[27]

With the Shakespeare Folio, Sankey is not a particularly assiduous expurgator, though he read carefully enough to correct an erroneous stage direction in *1 Henry IV*: at 3.3.51, the F2 stage direction reads "Enter Hotspurre," which he correctly changed to "Hostesse." For the most part, though, what caught his attention were obvious sexual innuendoes and blatant anti-Catholic references, like Lavatch's simile in *All's Well That Ends Well* of something fitting together as tightly as "the nun's lips to the friar's mouth" (2.2.20). But nineteen of the thirty-six plays are completely untouched, including *Two Gentleman of Verona* and *Romeo and Juliet*. In *Much Ado*, all that is marked out is the bawdy exchange between Margaret and Hero in 3.4 about women bearing "the weight of a man," and the similar sexual joking at the beginning of 5.2 between Margaret and Benedick, which ends with the phallic reference to "pikes" as "dangerous weapons for maids."

But *King John* is more rigorously censored, with John's confident claim to rule as "under heaven as supreme head" deleted as well as his sharp dismissal of the Pope's "usurped authority," along with John's vilification of the "corrupted" sale of pardons. Even the account of John's death is expurgated: Hubert announces that " the king, I fear, is poisoned," but Sankey has blotted out the concluding phrase asserting that the deed was undertaken "by a monk" (5.6.23, and again at l. 29). If Shakespeare was a secret Catholic, or a Catholic sympathizer, or even a more or less disinterested observer, it wasn't obvious to an admittedly interested near-contemporary Catholic reader; but the play can't quite be turned into the Protestant polemic of its sources, as revealed by the fact that the official allows the play at all.

The play ends with John murdered, and England unified, but under another child king, the young Henry, to whom the Bastard pledges his "faithful services/And true subjection everlastingly" (5.7.104–5) and offers his sanguine moralizing of what has happened:

> This England never did, nor never shall,
> Lie at the proud foot of a conqueror

But when it first did help to wound itself.
Now these her princes are come home again,
Come the three corners of the world in arms,
And we shall shock them. Nought shall make us rue
If England to itself do rest but true.

(5.7.112–18)

No doubt many in Shakespeare's audience in the mid 1590s would have heard this as a stirring appeal to national unity in the face of a threatened invasion from Catholic Spain. Indeed the Bastard's sentiments reveal exactly this context. The language and the logic come, as is so often the case in the histories, from Holinshed's *Chronicles*: "This little Iland, God having so bountifullie bestowed his blessings vpon it, that except it prooue false within it selfe, no treason whatsoeuer can preuaile against it."[28] This, however, as Lily B. Campbell was first to notice,[29] is taken not from Holinshed's section on the reign of King John in the early thirteenth century, but from the chronicler's account of the treason trial of the Jesuit priest Edmund Campion in 1581, which condemned the "horrible treasons" of the Catholic conspirators, motivated by the papal bull excommunicating Elizabeth and putting the godly nation at risk.

In its repurposing of Holinshed's providential patriotism for the end of *King John*, we might possibly have a telling piece of evidence against the view that Shakespeare was a secret Catholic sympathizer, but, whatever it means in his play for England to "rest but true," it is still not quite enough to identify him with some of the shrill anti-Catholic voices that could be heard. If Shakespeare wished only to assert the need for national unity in the face of an external Catholic threat and the fear of internal Catholic subversion, surely he would have allowed England's recovered strength to defeat the French, or at least, as in the anonymous *Troublesome Reign of King John*, have made the Dauphin sue for peace aware that England's renewed unity has dashed his hopes.[30]

That is, of course, exactly what the Bastard thinks has happened at the end of the play. Salisbury tells him that the French King is "[w]ith purpose presently to leave this war," and the Bastard replies: "He will the rather do it when he sees/Ourselves well-sinewed to our own defence." But Salisbury denies the simple, self-assured patriotism: "Nay, 'tis in a manner done already." The French King has "put his cause and quarrel/To the disposing of the Cardinal,/With whom yourself, myself, and other lords,/If you think meet, this afternoon will post/To consummate this business happily." Not England's recovered unity but "the disposing of the Cardinal" brings about the unexpected peace, and the Bastard quickly bows to necessity: "Let it be so" (5.7.86–96). The Cardinal's manipulations have ensured the Church's continued role in English affairs, perhaps a worrisome indication of the vulnerability of the proud Erastianism of Protestant England that John had anticipated, but perhaps also a fulfillment of some of Catholic England's dreams—some welcome recognition that in the 1590s an England completely "true" to itself would need to transcend the sectarian differences on which it depended to define itself.[31]

King John, however, was not the only play that drew the extended attention of Father Sankey at Vallodolid. The other play that is heavily marked by the Jesuit college official is, perhaps unsurprisingly, *Henry VIII*. Modern critics have often been drawn to the play's ecumenical spirit, especially in its dignified treatment of Queen Katherine, and to its irenic understanding—or maybe its *ironic* understanding—of what seems certainly the play's intended title, *All Is True*, before the play was hijacked for the group of Histories by Heminges and Condell in 1623. The play's complicated balancing is made overt in that the words "reformed" and "reformation" are spoken by Catholic voices, as Gordon McMullan has noted, as terms for the restraint of Protestant heresy.[32]

Father Sankey, however, found the play's staging of the Henrician Reformation not quite ecumenical enough for his seminary students. For them what would have been most unacceptable was its flattering treatment of Cranmer and Elizabeth. Positive adjectives applied to the archbishop are therefore expunged. From the second gentleman's comment about Bishop Gardiner, "He of Winchester/Is held no good lover of the Archbishop's,/The virtuous Cranmer" (4.1.103–5), Sankey blots out the final half-line appositive. Even in Henry's support for Cranmer, as he urges his nobles to "respect" the archbishop and "use him well," adding "he's worthy of it" (5.2.187–8), Sankey deletes this relatively muted assertion of Cranmer's merit. But it is mainly Cranmer's prophecy that sets

Sankey to work on his expurgation. More than half of the speech's forty-nine lines are inked out. The praise of Elizabeth's "wisdom and fair virtue," her "pure soul," her "Holy and heavenly thoughts" (5.5.24–33) are all found unfit to be read by the seminarians, as is the claim that in her reign "God shall be truly known, and those about her/From her shall read the perfect way of honour" (5.5.36–7). And all that remains of Cranmer's proleptic eulogy, "[b]ut she must die./She must, the saints must have her. Yet a virgin,/A most unspotted lily, shall she pass to th' ground/And all the world shall mourn her" (5.5.59–62), is merely the terse facticity of "but she must die."

The anti-Catholicism of *King John* and the pro-Protestantism of *Henry VIII* led a Catholic official to strike out passages in both.[33] Of course this tells us nothing about what Shakespeare believed or what he intended. It does not prove Shakespeare was anti-Catholic or pro-Protestant. Indeed the very fact that local censorship is both necessary and still capable of allowing the plays to be safely read by seminary students might well argue he was neither. Shakespeare could have made both plays less ambiguous. Certainly there were polemical models in both cases readily at hand. Father Sankey wasn't trying to have his students recognize in Shakespeare the capacious moral imagination and the suppleness of thought that we have come to value; but seemingly he did think it was worthwhile for his students to read the plays, just as long as they could be read in texts that would not undermine what the seminarians were being officially taught. "All things that are written are written for our doctrine" (*quaecumque scripta sunt ad nostram doctrinam scripta sunt*), says St Paul in Romans 15, but sometimes only with a little help. Even these two plays can be saved for seminary readers by relatively minor expurgation.

One play, however, needed even more radical handling. *Measure for Measure* is completely razored out. Pages F1ʳ to G6ᵛ have been excised, leaving only short stubs remaining in the volume. Razoring out sections of books was a common form of censorship, removing an offending section while leaving the majority of the book intact. Unfortunately Father Sankey left no note to explain why this play could not be treated as he did the others.[34] In the case of the eight pages on the Gunpowder Plot excised from Speed's *Historie* (see p. 62) it is obvious enough what motivated it. Here we can only guess at what made *Measure for Measure* unacceptable to Sankey, unsuitable to be read at all, rather than merely to be expurgated locally.

Perhaps it was simply the play's inescapable sexuality. It is, after all, a play set in motion by the Duke's efforts to restrain the city's sexual appetites, seemingly impossible without some master plan to "geld and splay all the youth of the city" (2.1.227–8). The play's high-minded concerns with justice and mercy work themselves out in a spacious field of sexual desire, whether it is that of the properly contracted Juliet and Claudio or the unruly passions of the customers of Mistress Overdone's brothel.

Sankey might have been able to censor the most obvious of the play's bawdy jokes, removing lines that might suggest Shakespeare's "lenity to lechery" (3.2.94), in Lucio's words. If Antonio's offer to spare Claudio in exchange for Isabella's willingness "to lay down the treasures of [her] body" (2.4.96) might have survived the expurgation in the conventionality of the phrasing, much of the fervid imagery of her refusal might well have been blotted out.

> Th'impression of keen whips I'd wear as rubies
> And strip myself to death as to a bed
> That longing have been sick for, ere I'd yield
> My body up to shame.

> (2.4.101–4)

Whips, rubies, strip, bed, longing, body, shame: as the old academic joke has it: "and this is Isabella saying 'no.'" Certainly the difficulty of defending "the deceit" of the bed-trick "from reproof" (3.1.258–9) must have been obvious, as Isabella in effect becomes a procuress for Angelo, although the similar scene in *All's Well* is untouched in the Valladolid Folio. But it would be impossible to remove the issue of sexuality itself, as it is the motor of Vienna's behavior throughout the play, though this could be a concern as much for "precise" Puritan readers as for Catholic ones.[35]

It is worth noting that familiar forms of anti-Catholicism find no significant voice in the play. Friar Thomas and Friar Peter are virtuous and respectfully treated, and the convent is a place for disciplined idealists, for "fasting maids, whose minds are dedicate/To nothing temporal" (2.2.155–6). Indeed it is only Lucio's cynicism about their virtue being real that the play holds up for criticism. Perhaps Angelo's experience of his distracted prayers as "Heaven in my mouth,/As if I did but only chew his name" (2.4.4–5) might have seemed too suggestive of eucharistic controversies to survive Sankey's deletions, but this is exactly the kind of local reference that throughout the volume is effectively subjected to his censoring pen.

There are, however, religious issues that are less tractable, and that, no less than the play's texture of sexuality, would justify the excision of *Measure for Measure* from the Valladolid Folio. This is a play about a duke disguising himself as a friar with the help of vowed clergy, hearing confessions, arranging a sexual encounter for an unmarried couple, and proposing to a young woman in a novitiate's habit, willfully ignoring her commitment to celibacy. I wish the pages of the Folio still existed; I suspect they would show Sankey beginning diligently to delete individual offensive passages until the hopelessness of the task of making the play acceptable made him reach for his razor.

The major problem, I would think, stems from the decision of the Duke not only to adopt the habit of a friar, pretending to be "a brother/of a gracious order, late come from the See/In special business from his Holiness" (3.2.212–14), but also, and more disturbingly, to *act* as if he were in fact ordained. It is not just the pretense; it is the presumption. In 2.3, he arrives at the prison, announcing himself to the Provost:

> Bound by my charity and my blessed order,
> I come to visit the afflicted spirits
> Here in the prison. Do me the common right
> To let me see them, and to make me know
> The nature of their crimes, that I may minister
> To them accordingly.
>
> (2.3.3–8)

If his disguise was merely a ruse to get him into the prison to talk with Claudio and Juliet that would be one thing, a highly charged but basically familiar comic device; but here he does "minister to them accordingly," a much more unsettling fact. Canon law prohibits laymen from taking confession and absolving sin, and the Duke's actions will keep the penitents he shrives from confessing to an

ordained priest, who would have the power of absolution. This position was definitively formulated at the fourteenth session of the
Council of Trent (1551):

> But as respects the minister of this sacrament [penance], the holy
> synod declares all these doctrines to be false and utterly alien from
> the truth of the Gospel, which perniciously extended the ministry of
> the keys to any other men soever, besides bishops and priests; sup-
> posing that those words of our Lord...were in such wise addressed
> indifferently and indiscriminately to all the faithful of Christ, as that
> everyone has the power of remitting sins, contrary to the institution
> of this sacrament, public sins, to wit, by rebuke, provided he that is
> rebuked shall acquiesce, but secret sins by a voluntary confession
> made to any person soever.[36]

The Duke, however, acts as if he has "the power of remitting sins."
Initially he asks Friar Thomas for a habit and instruction "How I may
formally in person bear/Like a true friar" (1.3.47–8) in order to observe
Angelo "in th'ambush of [the Duke's] name" (1.3.41) bring to heel the
moral laxity of Vienna, which his own permissiveness had encouraged.
He tells the Friar, however, that he has "[m]ore reasons for this action"
(1.3.48) than the two he admits (i.e. bringing about civic reform without risking his own good will and providing himself the opportunity
to discover, in the case of Angelo, "what our seemers be," 1.3.54),
although he never gets around to saying what his other "reasons" are.
Apparently, however, one is the desire to test the proposition that secular authority properly attired carries with it priestly powers. Perhaps
the cowl may make the monk.

The Duke gratuitously instructs Juliet to confess, acting his role
better than Friar Lawrence performs his legitimate ministerial one
in *Romeo and Juliet*. The Duke promises to teach this Juliet "how
[she] should arraign [her] conscience/And try [her] penitence, if it
be sound/Or hollowly put on" (2.3.21–3). The once lax Duke
reveals himself a severe cleric. He inquires whether the sexual
encounter that impregnated Juliet was "mutually committed"
(2.3.27), but once assured it was, he tells her that her sin was "of
heavier kind than [Claudio's]." And Juliet accepts the judgment,
willingly admitting her "heavier" guilt: "I do confess it, and repent
it, father" (2.3.28).[37]

But this is not enough. The Duke takes his disguise very seriously. Not content with pastoral care but insisting on theological rigor, he presses still harder on the idea of repentance. He tries to get Juliet to see some distinction between kinds of repentence, perhaps seeking to invoke, if the syntax were less convoluted and the sentence complete, a subtle and perhaps inadequately understood theological distinction between contrition for sin motivated either by fear of God's punishment or shame at one's actions, "[w]hich sorrow is always toward ourselves, not heaven" (2.3.32), and true repentance, which would be motivated only by the love of what God's grace promises or at least by an unwillingness further to offend a God whose love for us is so great.

Juliet neither completely comprehends the intended distinction, if it is intelligible, nor fully embraces it, replying ambiguously: "I do repent me as it is an evil./And take the shame with joy." The Duke seems to realize that this is the best he will get and quickly cuts off further conversation. "There rest," says the Duke, that is, "continue of that opinion," as the Arden editor glosses it; though it is not quite clear that her opinion is anything at all like the one the Duke has just tried to articulate. And in any case, perhaps out of his own frustration, he then immediately unsettles any possibility that her confession might bring her comfort: "Your partner, as I hear, must die tomorrow,/And I am going with instruction to him./Grace go with you, *Benedicte*" (2.3.35–9).

It must sound like absolution,[38] even if the news of Claudio's imminent death must trouble her repose. From Juliet's perspective, she has shown contrition and confessed to a theologically sophisticated if unsympathetic friar, who is apparently capable of absolving her sin. In act 4, scene 1, the Duke similarly assures Mariana that the bedtrick that will bring her to Angelo's side is "no sin,/Sith that the justice of your title to him/Doth flourish the deceit" (4.1.73–5). And in 4.3, he is ready to shrive Barnardine before his execution, and it is only Barnardine's stubborn refusal to confess, not any concern about the efficacy of his ministering, that leads the Duke to stop the execution. Indeed he seems confident in his ministry, frustrated only that Barnardine is "A creature unprepared, unmeet for death" (4.3.66).

For Father Sankey, that would be exactly the problem, for even had Barnardine confessed to the Duke, he would still be "unprepared," because the Duke does not have the ability to prepare him. Sacraments may function *ex opere operato*, but sacramental efficacy is transmitted through an ordained priest. When Angelo orders Claudio to be executed, he says, "Bring him his confessor; let him be prepared" (2.1.35), and, though the Duke uncomfortably prepares him to face the certainty of his death, he cannot prepare Claudio's soul for judgment. The Duke is no "confessor" and is unable to effect the absolution of those who have confessed to him, unless, of course, his actions can be read as evidence of the priesthood of all believers, a central Protestant notion, which the decree of the Council of Trent (see p. 68) was determined to deny.

Milton, however, voiced the reformers' understanding, insisting that "all Christians ought to know, that the title of Clergy S. *Peter* gave to all Gods people, till Pope *Higinus* and the succeeding Prelates took it from them, appropriating that name to themselves and their Priests only."[39] More explicitly, Thomas Cartwright, writing about the instruction in the Epistle of James (James 5:16) to "Knowledge your faultes one to another," sharply notes that the writer "says not one lay man vnto a Preeste," or even "one Parishioner vnto his owne Curate"; and Cartwright uses the biblical verse as authority for the idea that he "may as well make [his] confession to any other man" as to a member of the clergy since confession must really be made to God.[40] On the same grounds, Thomas Bell, noting that "we generally confess our selues sinners to our neighbors," justified the practice since Christ "in saying (these words) confes one to another, he commaundeth no more to make confession to a priest, then to a lay man: for he addeth forthwith, and pray for one an other that ye may be saued."[41]

But the administrator of a training college for Catholic priests could hardly endorse either the interpretation of the verse in the Epistle of James or the actions of the Duke in the play. Most of the time the Duke is disguised as a friar and ministering to the community as if he were one,[42] a role too intricately woven into the fabric of the plot to be disentangled and removed. What needs to be removed is the play itself, as the stubs deforming the Valladolid Folio attest.

They don't, of course, prove that the play is anti-Catholic. They prove only that a Catholic official at a Jesuit college in the 1640s could find no way to expurgate it so it would be suitable to be read by future priests. Still, the Valladolid Folio makes it a bit harder to credit readings of the play designed to prove Shakespeare's Catholic sympathies, since a Catholic, who apparently admired Shakespeare (and might even have provided the Folio copy to the Library), seems to have been unable to see them.

Nonetheless, if Sankey's razor in this case seemed the best remedy to keep Shakespeare safe for seminarians, the play itself is neither assertively anti-Catholic nor pro-Protestant. It doesn't seem polemical at all. To whatever degree it is capable of achieving a happy ending, *Measure for Measure* depends on recognizing and rehabilitating our compromised commitments, not to the doctrines of any Church but to one another.

This is a fallen world with obviously flawed inhabitants, even—perhaps especially—the Duke, and the play pointedly, unlike most of the other comedies, provides no temporary "green world" as a clarifying alternative, just the "moated grange" (3.1.265) in which Mariana and Angelo will consummate their betrothal in terms deeply humiliating to both. In this play the recalcitrance of fallen nature does not yield as easily as it does in other comedies to desire—either of the characters or our own. The comedy itself, if that is what *Measure for Measure* is, demands, as Mariana suggests in her psychologically implausible love of Angelo, only our belief in the possibility of a happy ending "moulded out of faults" (5.1.437).[43]

The title, *Measure for Measure*, might easily suggest "an eye for an eye," a rigorous code of justice where crime merits an equivalent punishment, or as the play poses it:

> An Angelo for a Claudio; death for death.
> Haste still pays haste, and leisure answers leisure;
> Like doth quit like, and measure still for measure.
>
> (5.1.407–9)

This is how Shakespeare uses the phrase elsewhere: "Measure for measure must be answered," says Warwick, brutally promising to replace the severed head of York with that of his murderer, Clifford (*3 Henry VI*, 2.6.55). But the biblical allusion from Matthew 7:1 (and Luke 6:37) suggests a somewhat different meaning: "Judge not that ye be not judged, for with what judgement ye judge, ye shall bee judged, and with what measure ye mete, it shall be measured to you againe." If Nietzsche thought that no principle of justice at all but only a faint-hearted prudence,[44] Christians hear it differently. God's justice must be rigorous; ours must be less severe, if only from the knowledge of our own sinfulness: "And why seest thou the mote that is in thy brother's eye and perceyuest not the beame that is in thine owne eye?"

This seems to me the modest ethical argument of Shakespeare's play. "He who the sword of heaven will bear/Should be as holy as severe" (3.2.254–5), says the Duke, but both adjectives, the play insists, must be heavily qualified. It is not that the law can be enforced only by the saintly. It is that the law's severity must be tempered by the knowledge of the near impossibility of saintliness. Both the sins of the sinners and the sins of the would-be saints are on display here. The ameliorating logic of the play itself is held up for inspection. The Duke would justify his deceptions by what they bring about: "the doubleness of the benefit defends the deceit from reproof" (3.1.258–9). But if this sounds awfully close to some notion that the ends justify the means, well, maybe they do.

Certainly there is something disappointing about the end of the play. There is none of the joyful sense of earned fulfillment for the lovers, or some larger intuition that there is "mirth in heaven,/ When earthly things made even/Atone together" (*As You Like It*, 5.1.106–8). But then this is not *As You Like It*. This is life as we usually experience it, with our dreams and desires incompletely satisfied or unfulfilled, or, what is worse, satisfied and unfulfilling. Comedy is usually more fully responsive to human desire and design than life is.[45] But not here. Here we are forced to recognize that comic triumph is not innocuous: event will not yield to desire without some other desire yielding to event. There is little sense of celebration; at best there is relief.

The three disrupted betrothals will be completed, but none with innocent happiness, and, in a scene that troubles almost everyone, the Duke would find a mate to join the pairings. In spite of his claim to be immune to "the dribbling dart of love" (1.3.2), he proposes to Isabella, compelled by her "goodness" (3.1.181), though she has given no sign of any romantic interest in him and the austere terms in which her goodness has revealed itself could hardly suggest otherwise. Seemingly the proposal troubles Isabella. At least she is not obviously compelled by it. Revealing that Claudio, feared dead, is indeed safe, the Duke says to her, "Give me your hand and say you will be mine./He is my brother too." There must be an awkward pause, a very awkward pause, as she remains silent, before he relents: "but fitter time for that" (5.1.490–1). And then at the end, as she still stands unpromisingly in her novitiate's habit, he again proposes: "Dear Isabel,/I have a motion much imports your good;/Whereto if you'll a willing ear incline,/What's mine is yours, and what is yours is mine." But again she doesn't answer, and again he must deflect the awkwardness: "So bring us to our palace, where we'll show/What's yet behind, that's meet you all should know" (5.1.531–6). Perhaps Isabella signals her acceptance nonverbally, and together they lead everyone off the stage—or perhaps not. I saw a production in Budapest several years ago where Isabella reached into her handbag, removed a small pistol, and shot herself.

But what I take to be the point of Shakespeare's scripting of the scene is that the Duke indeed intends the conditional in his "If you'll a willing ear incline," certainly hoping she will so incline but, unlike Angelo, unwilling to coerce her acceptance. Her silence perhaps conveys her ambivalence about leaving the convent, or her ambivalence about the Duke, or maybe even her inexpressible delight at this surprising turn of events—but, if it is this last, it is something shallower than anything that Shakespeare anywhere else would call love. A "present and perfect Consent," said the ecclesiastical lawyer Henry Swinburne, "alone maketh Matrimony,"[46] in the process of making a series of subtle legal distinctions about matrimonial law, but arguably it is a present and perfect consent that alone makes comedies something other than problem plays. *Measure for Measure* is, however, decidedly a problem play, where consent, as Angelo and Lucio discover, might be neither present nor perfect, and whatever Isabella's silence means for her, it also serves to mark the limit of the Duke's ability to turn this recalcitrant material into present or perfect comedy—as well as the limits of Shakespeare's intention to do so.[47] On the other hand, we should not forget that it is only through the Duke's frantic manipulations, along with the provost's timely recollection of the convenient death of Ragazone, that the play avoids becoming tragic.

Shakespeare made the play Catholic in his changes to his source, *Promos and Cassandra*, placing Isabella in the convent, letting the Duke assume his disguise as Friar Lodowick, and even by moving the action to Vienna (if indeed he is responsible for that),[48] but Catholicism is finally no more what the play is about than it is what *Two Gentleman of Verona* is about, though of course matters of religion are so much more unavoidable here. But, as many have noted, Catholic Vienna (or perhaps Catholic Ferrara) in the play is not really very different from Protestant London, their similarity established not least in the way Isabella and Angelo enact parallel Catholic and "precise" (1.3.50; 3.1.93) versions of moral rigor revealing itself as a form of spiritual pride.[49] Both versions would effect an impossible reformation of human behavior, ignoring that it is *human*. Sex will always happen and is likely often to be disruptive: "it is impossible to extirp it quite," says Lucio, "till eating and drinking be put down" (3.2.98–9). With his razor, Father Sankey was able at least to "extirp it quite" from the Folio, along with everything else in *Measure for Measure*, a play that could not help but disturb a mid-seventeenth-century Jesuit in charge of an English college in Spain for the training of priests.

But *Measure for Measure* apparently didn't disturb King James when it was played at Whitehall on 26 December 1604. James would have been unlikely to recognize himself in either the hypocritical Angelo or the improvising Duke, however much Angelo's simile of the Duke appearing "like power divine" (5.1.367) might have gratified James's absolutist fantasies. The play itself, however, seems unlikely to have done so,[50] though that says little about whether the King enjoyed it. *Comedy of Errors, Love's Labor's Lost, The Merry Wives of Windsor, Henry V,* and *The Merchant of Venice* were also among the fourteen plays presented at court that winter. The only one we know he liked was *Merchant*; he requested a second performance two days after the first, but of course that play has a Duke who is so much less "fantastical" (4.3.156). Still, *Measure for Measure* passed without royal comment, and in fact with almost no contemporary comment of any sort. Certainly no one in England seems to have felt the need for a razor, in spite of a play that could be as offensive to English Puritans as to Catholics. But maybe that's the point.

Now scholars, in what is probably the predictable "tock" to the "tick" of confessionalization, have begun to focus more on what joined Christians in early modern England rather than on what divided them. The "big-tent" Christianity, which critics of an earlier generation had somewhat casually assumed about early modern religious sensibilities,[51] may indeed be closer to the truth about most or at least many people's lived religion in early modern England than the distinctive and divisive confessionalism emphasized by the granular revisionism of recent years. Although Jesus claimed that he had "come to put fire on the earth" (Luke 12:49), it seems certain that most English people were eager to understand this only as a metaphor and to hear Thomas Middleton's question as happily rhetorical: "Are not the Flesh-eating fires quenched, and our Faggots conuerted to gentler uses?"[52]

James would write from Edinburgh to an understandably curious Cecil, that although he would be reluctant to see Catholics in England "multiplie," he was unwilling "that the bloode of any man shall be shedde for diuersitie in opinions of religion."[53] By 1604, the year *Measure for Measure* was written, the new king would regularly voice his desire for what he called "one mutuall Christendome," his hopes for union clearly conceived more inclusively than just a political union of Scotland and England, seeking rather, as he said, "a generall Christian vnion in Religion."[54] He was no doubt thinking of a union of European states in large part to resist the growing Ottoman threat. But his appeal for a "settled amitie" between Catholic and Protestant and his desire for a broad Church of the Protestant faithful would have been satisfactory to the large part of the English nation. Most people knew little about the great matters of state and the nice points of theology, and their daily experience would have usually led them to accept that they had more in common than not and to understand that everyone had most to gain at least by acting as if that were so.[55]

Confessional differences have been overstated, or, rather, the daily impact of those differences has been overstated. "Religion is Christianity," Donne wrote to a friend: "You know I never fettered nor imprisoned the word Religion; not straightning it Frierly, ad *Religiones factitias*, (as the *Romans* call well their orders of Religion) nor immuring it in a *Rome*, or a *Wittemberg* [*sic*], or a *Geneva*; they are all virtuall beams of one Sun..."[56] For many other English people it was the same. Hobbes would later write in *Behemoth*:

> I confess I know very few Controversies amongst Christians of points
> necessary to Salvation; they are the Questions of Authority and
> Power over the *Church*, or of Profit, or Honour to *Church-men*, that for
> the most part raise all the Controversies. For what man is he that will
> trouble himself, and fall out with his Neighbours for the saving of my
> Soul, or the Soul of any other than himself.[57]

Maybe this is just evidence of what a convert might be eager to
believe and of what someone writing a generation later might
imagine to have once been true; but more likely it points to a
continuity of amicable, unsystematic religious thought in which
communal harmony regularly trumped doctrinal purity, allowing a Christian commonality to be discovered in what Debora
Shuger has called "a minimalist version of saving faith."[58] While
for zealous Protestants and fervent Catholics theological positions were always intensely felt and exclusive, for most of England religion was normally a more expansive field of piety and
social connection. Maybe all roads don't lead to Rome—or away
from it. As the decidedly worldly Lucio says, "Grace is grace, despite
of controversy."[59]

Notes

1 See Patrick Cheney, *Shakespeare, National Poet-Playwright* (Cambridge:
  Cambridge University Press, 2004); and Michael Dobson, *The Making of
  a National Poet: Shakespeare, Adaptation, and Authorship, 1660–1769* (Oxford:
  Oxford University Press, 1992).

2 The play does not have a single source for the plot, but the story of the
  courtship of Julia and Proteus derives from Jorge de Montemayor's *La
  Diana*, published initially in Spanish in 1542, but which Shakespeare
  may well have known from a French translation published in 1569, or
  possibly from an English translation done in 1582, though not published
  until 1598.

3 Maurice Hunt, on the contrary, has argued provocatively that the comedy is completed only as "certain Protestant ideas displace, or supersede,
  certain Catholic terms presented earlier in the play." See his *Shakespeare's
  Religious Allusiveness: Its Play and Tolerance* (Aldershot: Ashgate, 2004), 13.

4 See, for example, Richard Wilson, "A World Elsewhere: Shakespeare's
  Sense of an Exit," *Proceedings of the British Academy*, vol. 117, ed. F. M. L.
  Thompson (Oxford: Oxford University Press for the British Academy,
  2002), 165–99.

5 Ascham, *The Scholemaster* (London, 1570), sig. H4ᵛ, F1ᵛ.

6 Brooke, *The Tragicall Historye of Romeus and Iuliet* (London, 1562), sig. ¶3ʳ.

7 Brooke, sig. ¶2ʳ–3ᵛ.

8 Greene, *The Spanish Masquerado* (London, 1589), sig. A3ᵛ.

9 Martin Luther, "Lectures on Galatians," in *Luther's Works*, eds. Jaroslav Pelikan and Helmut Lehmann (St Louis, MO: Concordia, 1963), vol. 26, 140.

10 On 5 October 1538, Cranmer wrote to Cromwell that "as the Grey Friars, Canterbury, is very commodious for my servant, Thomas Cobham, brother to Lord Cobham, I beg you will help him to the said house." See *Letters and Papers, Foreign and Domestic, of the Reign of Henry VIII*, ed. James Gairdner (London: H M Stationary Office, 1893), vol. 13 (2), 537.

11 *Tudor Royal Proclamations*, eds. Paul L. Hughes and James F. Larkin (New Haven, CT and London: Yale University Press, 1969), vol. 3, 91, 90.

12 "An Acte against Jesuites, Semynarie Priestes and such other Sundrie Persons," in *Statutes of the Realm* (London, 1819), vol. 4, 706–7. See also Christopher Haigh, "The Continuity of Catholicism in the English Reformation," *The English Reformation Revised*, ed. Christopher Haigh (Cambridge: Cambridge University Press, 1987), 176–208, who questions whether, under these proscriptive legal conditions, Catholic missionaries to England properly constitute a "Counter Reformation," arguing instead that "it was less a spiritual crusade and more a series of adjustments to the fact of disestablishment" (p. 178).

13 E. K. Chambers, *The Elizabethan Stage* (Oxford: Clarendon Press, 1923), vol. 4, 306, includes a letter written from the Privy Council to the Archbishop of Canterbury in 1589, "to require" the players to submit their playbooks to a review of "the matters of their comedyes and tragedyes" and order the licensors "to stryke out and reform suche partes and matters as they shall fynd unfytt and undecent to be handled in playes." The second quoted phrase above is cited from the York *Court Book, 1575–1580*, in Harold C. Gardiner, *Mysteries' End: An Investigation of the Last Days of the Medieval Religious Stage* (New Haven, CT: Yale University Press, 1946), 78.

14 Quoted in Gerald Bentley, *The Jacobean and Caroline Stage* (Oxford and New York: Oxford University Press, 1941), vol. 1, 277. The performance attracted notice because it was seen to be "in contempt of the ceremonies of the Church" (i.e. the English Laudian Church), which was widely criticized by Puritan opponents for its restoration of forms of worship that seemed to backslide toward Catholic practices. See *Calendar of State Papers, Domestic Series, of the Reign of Charles I, 1639*, eds. John Bruce, W. D. Hamilton, and Mrs. S. C. Lomas (London, 1871), 140–1.

15 Peter Lake, "Anti-Popery: The Structure of a Prejudice," in *Conflict in Early Stuart England: Studies in Religion and Politics 1603–1642*, eds. Richard Cust and Ann Hughes (London: Longman, 1989), vol. 14, 74.

16 *Proceedings in Parliament 1614*, ed. Maija Jansson (Philadelphia, PA: American Philosophical Society, 1988), 7.

17 Joseph Hall, *The Works of Joseph Hall, D.D.* (London: Oxford University Press, 1837), vol. 5, 10. Similarly, a zealous Thomas Taylor warns his flock: "Wee must depart from needlesse association and assistance: how can we strike hands, and embrace amitie and societie with those who have broken off from God?" See Taylor, *Two Sermons* (London, 1624), sig. C2ᵛ.

18 For the most eloquent account of the trauma of the Reformation and the resilience of Catholicism in early modern England, see Eamon Duffy, *The Stripping of the Altars: Traditional Religion in England c.1400–c. 1580* (New Haven, CT and London: Yale University Press, 1992).

19 See Peter Lake, "Religious Identities in Shakespeare's England," in *A Companion to Shakespeare*, ed. David Scott Kastan (Oxford: Blackwell, 1999), 57–84; Patrick Collinson, "The Politics of Religion and the Religion of Politics in Elizabethan England," *Historical Research* 82 (2009), 74–92; Christopher Haigh's *The Plain Man's Pathways to Heaven: Kinds of Christianity in Post-Reformation England* (Oxford: Oxford University Press, 2007); Michael C. Questier, *Catholicism and Community in Early Modern England: Politics, Aristocratic Patronage, and Religion, c.1550–1640* (Cambridge: Cambridge University Press, 2006); Ethan Shagan (ed.), *Catholics and the "Protestant" Nation: Religious Politics and Identity in Early Modern England* (Manchester and New York: Manchester University Press, 2005); Norman L. Jones, *The English Reformation: Religion and Cultural Adaptation* (Oxford: Blackwell, 2002); Alexandra Walsham, *Church Papists: Catholicism, Conformity and Confessional Polemic in Early Modern England*, 2nd edn. (London: Boydell and Brewer, 1999).

20 Anthony Milton, "A Qualified Intolerance: the Limits and Ambiguities of Early Stuart Anti-Catholicism," in *Catholicism and Anti-Catholicism in Early Modern English Texts*, ed. Arthur F. Marotti (New York: St Martin's Press, 1999), 105.

21 On Bale's relation to Thomas Cromwell and Richard Morison, as well as for a fuller account of his play's revisionary historiography, see my "'Holy Wurdes' and 'Slypper Wit': John Bale's *King Johan* and the Poetics of Propaganda," in *Rethinking the Henrician Era: Essays on Early Tudor Texts and Contexts*, ed. Peter C. Herman (Urbana and Chicago, IL: University of Illinois Press, 1994), 267–82.

22 *The Dramatic Works of Colley Cibber, Esq., in Five Volumes* (London, 1777), vol. 5, 240–1.

23 Cibber, *The Dramatic Works*, 241.

24 The copy was sold by the College to the Folger Library in May of 1928 for £1000, a private sale handled by Maggs Brothers. The significance of the volume was first brought to general notice by Roland Mushat Frye, in his *Shakespeare and Christian Doctrine* (Princeton, NJ: Princeton University Press, 1963) in an appendix entitled "The Roman Catholic

Censorship of Shakespeare", 275–94. I thank Georgianna Ziegler of the Folger Library for her help in reconstructing the Folio's journey to the Folger collection.

25 See Msgr. Michael E. Williams, "The Library at Saint Alban's English College Valladolid: Censorship and Acquisitions," *Recusant History* 26 (2002), 133, although he does not discuss the Shakespeare folio except to refer to it in a note as a book that the College "once possessed." I must thank Stephen Parks, the Librarian at the Elizabethan Club at Yale, for sharing with me his research on the books in Saint Alban's English College library.

26 See, for example, *The English College at Madrid, 1611–1767*, ed. Edwin Henson, (Leeds: J. Whitehead, printed for the Catholic Record Society, 1929), 35, 37, 43, 44, 49, 57, 73, 306, 311, 321.

27 Msgr. Michael E. Williams, "The Library at Saint Alban's English College Valladolid: Censorship and Acquisitions," 135.

28 Holinshed, *The Third Volume of Chronicles* (London, 1586), sig. 6L6ᵛ.

29 Campbell, *Shakespeare's Histories: Mirrors of Elizabethan Policy* (San Marino, CA: Huntington Library Press, 1947), 126. See also Jean-Christophe Mayer, *Shakespeare's Hybrid Faith: History, Religion and the Stage* (New York: Palgrave Macmillan, 2006), 96.

30 See my " 'To Set a Form upon that Indigest': Shakespeare's Fictions of History," *Comparative Drama* 17 (1983), esp. 8–16.

31 See Mayer, *Shakespeare's Hybrid Faith*, esp. 95–101; and also Jeffrey Knapp, *Shakespeare's Tribe: Church, Nation, and Theater in Renaissance England* (Chicago, IL: University of Chicago Press, 2002), 95–102.

32 In his Arden edition of *King Henry VIII* (London: Thomson, 2000), 408, note to lines 53, 54.

33 There is of course evidence of other Catholic readers of Shakespeare. Alison Shell has written a particularly suggestive account of what can be learned from these in her *Shakespeare and Religion* (London: Methuen Drama, 2010), esp. 79–119.

34 It is not, it must be said, certain that the excision was undertaken at the same time as the other expurgation, or even that it was done by Sankey, however likely it is; and there is no way to know for sure what motivated it. I am assuming that it was undertaken as part of his expurgation of the volume, but, in point of fact, it could have been otherwise. One of my students has suggested impishly that perhaps Sankey razored it out because he admired it so much that he wanted the copy for himself or to send to a friend. It is, of course, possible.

35 See Peter Lake with Michael Questier, *The Antichrist's Lewd Hat: Protestants, Papists and Players in Post-Reformation England* (New Haven, CT and London: Yale University Press, 2002), 621–700, who read the play as an "exercise in anti-puritanism" (p. 622).

36 See *Canons and Decrees of the Council of Trent*, trans. and ed. Theodore Alois Buckley (London: Routledge, 1851), 93.

37 N. W. Bawcutt in his edition of the play (Oxford: Oxford University Press, 1991), points out that George Whetstone, in his "Rare Historie of Promos and Cassandra," in *An Heptameron of Ciuill Discourses*, says the opposite: that "the man was held to be the greatest offender and therefore had the severest punishment" (sig. N2ᵛ), 135.

38 David Beauregard sees this scene as being "complete with the suggestion of final absolution when the Duke bids her 'Grace go with you, Benedicte,'" in "Shakespeare on Monastic Life: Nuns and Friars in *Measure for Measure*," in *Shakespeare and the Culture of Christianity in Early Modern England*, eds. Dennis Taylor and David N. Beauregard (New York: Fordham University Press, 2003), 327.

39 Milton, *The Reason of Church-Government Urg'd* (London, 1641), sig. G2ᵛ.

40 Cartwright, *Two Very Godly and Comfortable Letters* (London, 1589), 84 [but no page numbers or signatures are marked].

41 Thomas Bell, *The Suruey of Popery* (London, 1596), sig. Mm1ᵛ.

42 The Duke's behavior might be read as an example of temporal authority assuming a religious function even as it fulfills Protestant stereotypes about meddlesome friars, adding to its awkwardness for Father Sankey. See Debora Shuger's *Political Theologies in Shakespeare's England: The Sacred and the State in* Measure for Measure (Basingstoke: Palgrave, 2001).

43 Sarah Beckwith says that "What hope there is in this play lies in the forgiveness of women and the possibility that the best men might be molded out of faults." See her *Shakespeare and the Grammar of Forgiveness* (Ithaca, NY and London: Cornell University Press, 2011), 81.

44 F. W. Nietzsche, *The Antichrist*, trans. H. L. Mencken (New York: Knopf, 1920), 129: "What a notion of justice, of a 'just' judge!"

45 See my "*All's Well That Ends Well* and the Limits of Comedy," *ELH* 52 (1985), 575–89.

46 *A Treatise of Spousals, or Matrimonial Contracts* (London, 1686), 14. Swinburne died in 1624 and the *Treatise* was published posthumously.

47 John D. Cox notes the multiple silences at the end of the play in his *Seeming Knowledge: Shakespeare and Skeptical Faith* (Waco, TX: Baylor University Press, 2007), 61.

48 Gary Taylor has provocatively suggested that the play was set by Shakespeare in Ferrara, and that only in a later revision by Middleton was its setting moved to Vienna. See "Shakespeare's Mediterranean *Measure for Measure*," in *Shakespeare and the Mediterranean: The Selected Papers of the International Shakespeare Association World Congress, Valencia, 2001*, eds. Thomas Clayton, Susan Brock, and Vicente Forés (Newark, DE: University of Delaware Press, 2004), 243–69.

49 See Peter Lake (with Michael Questier), *The Antichrist's Lewd Hat: Protestants, Papists and Players in Post-Reformation England*, 675 and *passim*.

50 Some critics have, of course, argued the reverse, perhaps most notably Daryl Gless, *"Measure for Measure": the Law and the Convent* (Princeton, NJ: Princeton University Press, 1979).

51 See, for example, G. Wilson Knight, *The Christian Renaissance* (New York: W. W. Norton, 1962); Douglas Bush, *Prefaces to Renaissance Literature* (Cambridge, MA: Harvard University Press, 1965); and Roy Battenhouse, *Shakespearean Tragedy: Its Art and Christian Premises* (Bloomington, IN: University of Indiana Press, 1969).

52 Thomas Middleton, *The Peace-maker: or, Great Brittaines Blessing* (London, 1618), sig. B3ʳ.

53 *Correspondence of King James VI of Scotland with Sir Robert Cecil and Others in England*, ed. John Bruce (London: Camden Society, 1861), 36.

54 See James I, *The Workes of the Most High and Mighty Prince, Iames by the Grace of God, King of Great Britaine, France and Ireland, Defender of the Faith, &c.* (London, 1616), sig. Ss6ᵛ.

55 See Christopher Marsh's *Popular Religion in Sixteenth-Century England: Holding Their Peace* (Basingstoke and London: Macmillan, 1998).

56 In *Letters to Severall Persons of Honour Written by John Donne* (London, 1651), sig. E3ʳ. The address of the letter is printed as "*To Sir* H. R." but that is probably an error for "H. G.," Henry Goodere, Donne's close friend with whom he regularly corresponded.

57 Hobbes, *Behemoth, or an Epitome of the Civil Wars in England from 1640 to 1660* (London, 1679), sig. C8ʳ⁻ᵛ·

58 See Debora Shuger's essay on Sir John Harrington, "A Protesting Catholic Puritan in Elizabethan England," *Journal of British Studies* 48 (2009), 624; and also Jeffery Knapp's *Shakespeare's Tribe: Church Nation, and Theater in Renaissance England* (Chicago, IL and London: University of Chicago Press, 2002), which similarly finds in Harrington one example of "a reformist tradition...that elevated Christian fundamentals and fellowship over doctrinal precision and zeal" (p. 142).

59 Cf. Donne's remark in a letter to Goodere written in 1615 about "the sound true opinion, that in all Christian professions there is a way to salvation," *Letters to Severall Persons of Honour Written by John Donne*, sig. O2ᵛ.

4

Conversion and Cosmopolitism

> Human beings depend for their sense of identity on
> the reactions of those around them.
>
> Stanley Wells

For complex reasons, some of which have already been considered, religion in recent years has been enthusiastically recognized as one of the fundamental concerns expressed and explored in Shakespeare's plays. Nonetheless, for all the focus on Shakespeare and religion, "religion" as a category usually remains oddly undefined in these discussions. Perhaps this is with good reason. It seems to me to be one of those words, much like "art" or "politics" or "society," for which any definition will either include or exclude too much and inevitably clarify too little. In the main, I suppose, for most people religion involves something of what Mircea Eliade called "the experience of the sacred,"[1] or at least it names the social and imaginative space in which the sacred can be thought to intersect with and mark our quotidian lives. But a lot, I know, is neglected even in that broad definition and perhaps too much still allowed.

In early modern England, the points of intersections were inescapable. Religion had not yet been "privatized," if it has ever successfully been.[2] It existed as the essential medium in which the world was experienced and described. The "long, withdrawing roar" of "the Sea of Faith," which Matthew Arnold so clearly could hear in "Dover Beach," was heard, if it was noticed at all, as just a phase in the unrelenting tidal action of religious concern, which was the natural environment in which people lived.

Nonetheless, whatever "religion" denotes, and however much it is recognized as a means to register the sacred rather than seen to serve as an ideological mask to effect purely secular ends, in speaking about Shakespeare we have normally used the word as a term more or less coextensive with "Christianity." Historians of religion have taught us to see how inadequate the labels "Protestant" and "Catholic" are to describe the religious experience of the average believer in early modern England, but however complex, often contradictory, and exceptionally labile confessional faith was in the period, it was inevitably understood to be a "Christian" experience. But "religion," defined as I just have done (or, in truth, as I have tried to avoid doing), would obviously include many thoughts, beliefs, and actions that are not Christian at all.

A secularized modernity has found it easy, with the recognized plurality of religious experiences, to reify religion as a distinct category of understanding. Arguably, as a number of scholars have claimed, it is in the early modern period that this process begins, born from the opposition of the traditional faith and the reform, from the schismatic tendency of Protestantism itself, and from the growing awareness of a diversity of non-Christian beliefs as trade and colonization brought Europeans in contact with more of the world.[3]

The reification of "religion" is an effect, one could say, of its pluralization. The Catholic priest Thomas Alfield (Aufield) wrote anxiously, in his account of the execution of Edmund Campion, of "our natiue contrie, so devided dayly with numbers of newe faiths and religions."[4] Sixty years later a pamphleteer could give voice to the fear of England becoming so *"Amsterdamnified"* that "A man may with more facility reckon up all the species and kinds of Nature, then describe all the Sects, Divisions and Opinions in Religion that are at this time amongst us."[5] But there were also, as English readers would increasingly learn, religions elsewhere. William Biddulph's *The trauels of certaine Englishmen into Africa, Asia, Troy, Bythinia, Thracia, and to the Blacke Sea And into Syria, Cilicia, Pisidia, Mesopotamia, Damascus, Canaan, Galile, Samaria, Iudea, Palestina, Ierusalem, Iericho, and to the Red Sea: and to sundry other places* (London, 1612), spoke of "the diuersities of Religions in those countries" (sig. A2ᵛ). Edward Brereward systematized the growing anthropological knowledge into "four sorts or sects of Religion," i.e. "Idolatrie, *Mahumetanisme, Iudaisme,* and Christianity," that can be "obserued in the sundrie regions of the World."[6]

In the face of the unmistakable evidence of multiple religions, then, perhaps it was not such a very long way, as John Bossy has claimed, to get from "plurality as a problem which urgently required solution, to an abstractable essence of them, 'religion' in general..."[7]

I wonder, however, if the distance might not be significantly harder to bridge than Bossy imagines. At least in early modern England, the problem of the plural wasn't successfully solved by abstraction. It is not that it couldn't have been: it just wasn't. There are indeed many religions, as people increasingly were aware, but only one was thought to be true; that is, only one was thought really to be religion. From within any given individual's experience of the sacred, variant experience was inevitably seen as a mere "superstition" or a "false religion," and thus not really "religion" at all. In 1589, John Bate could write that "Although in the worlde there are sowed many and sundry faiths, that is to say religions, as that there is an *Indian* faith, a *Iewish* faith, a fayth of the *Mahometistes*, a faith of the *Georgians*, a Papisticall faithe: yet is there but one true Christian faith."[8] Similarly, Samuel Purchas, in his *Purchas His Pilgrimage: or, Relations of the World and the Religions Observed in all Ages and Places Discouered*, that extraordinary history of travel and exploration, would insist that "the true Religion can be but one," even as he admits as its very subject the multiple "other Religions" of the world. These, however, he sees as "but strayings" from the "true Religion," forms of what he calls "irreligious religion" in which "men wander in the darke, and in labyrinthes of errour."[9]

Of course, considered temporally, Protestantism is the "straying," but, in any case, an irreligious religion clearly doesn't deserve the noun. The oxymoron is self-cancelling (like Othello's "honourable murderer"), and Purchas's *Pilgrimage* may be thought to admit in its very title the exclusivity of its understanding. Like all pilgrimages, it has a certain destination; it is not a journey of discovery but of confirmation. What it seeks is the evidence of what it already knows to be true. It would still be a long time before Thomas Jefferson could say sanguinely that there are "probably a thousand different systems of religion" of which "ours is but one of that thousand," or for many to believe with him that "it does me no injury for my neighbour to say there are twenty gods, or no god."[10] Purchas didn't think this way. No one in Shakespeare's England did.

We are, however, used to seeing Shakespeare in his exceptionalism: he imagines what has been unimaginable and his imaginings help bring it about. "He wrote the text of modern life,"[11] said Emerson. But in this case I am not so sure; or, if it is true, it is not in the sense Emerson intended. I want to think about Shakespeare in relation to the "other religions" that Purchas saw as "but strayings" from the true one, but not all of "the thousand different systems of religion" that Jefferson would admit, but just the two, Judaism and Islam, with which Christianity shares a common culture as Abrahamic peoples of the book.

Of course their intertwined histories are not so simple or happy as that last inclusive phrase suggests. Baroni, Tancred's guide in Disraeli's 1847 novel, says that "The Arabs are only Jews on horseback,"[12] a sentimental encapsulation of an urgent problem that still haunts us. Christian Europe invents a bifold Semitic other—a nomadic Arab and a wandering Jew—as part of its own anxious efforts at self-definition, and in the process renders both Arab and Jewish histories largely invisible. The question, I suppose, is does Shakespeare resist or reproduce this invention.

It does not seem to me an accident that the two plays of Shakespeare that most urgently provoke the question are both set in Venice: on 22 July 1598, James Roberts entered *a booke of the Marchant of Venyce, or otherwise called the Jewe of Venyce*, while on 6 October 1621 Thomas Walkley entered and early the following year would publish *The Tragedie of Othello, the Moore of Venice*. We have *The Jew of Venice* and *The Moor of Venice*, two plays whose titles with their preposition seemingly claim something about the inclusiveness of the Republic, though interestingly the printed title of the 1600 quarto of *The Merchant of Venice* is somewhat less generously cosmopolitan[13] in its imagination of the story: *The most excellent Historie of the* Merchant of Venice. *With the extreame crueltie of Shylocke the Iewe towards the sayd Merchant.* Both the plays, with their distinctive exogenous figures, raise complex questions about how (or if) cultures can create coherent terms of community that can successfully include the alien presences that the cultures seem both to require and resist. They ask if that presence can really be *of* Venice rather than merely resident *in* it.

Venice was the place that seemed most inclusive, widely recognized as the most cosmopolitan of European cities. Thomas Coryate, a seventeenth-century English traveler, almost literalizes this in his account of the Rialto: "a man may very properly call it rather *Orbis* than *Vrbis forum*, that is, a marketplace of the world, not of the citie."[14] The Englishman found himself amazed by the "greatest magnificence of architecture to be seen, that any place vnder the sunne doth yeelde. Here may you both see all manner of fashions of attire, and heare all the languages of Christendome, besides those that are spoken by the barbarous Ethnickes" (sig. O7ʳ). But lurking in the oft-stated admiration for Venetian cosmopolitanism is a fear that its remarkable plenitude is inherently incoherent and unstable. This is the fear that Spenser, for example, in a dedicatory sonnet written for Lewis Lewkenor's translation of Gasparo Contarini's *The Commonwealth and Gouernment of Venice* (1599), admits in calling the city the "third" Babel, the unsettling successor to Rome and its predecessor, the biblical empire of Genesis 11, even as he insists that Venice is differentiated from both by its superior "policie of right" (sig. ⋆3ᵛ).

Shakespeare's Venice plays raise questions about what that policy is and in what sense it might be thought "right," engaging the question of cosmopolitanism as an effective answer to difference. A sophisticated political cosmopolitanism has recently been put forward by social theorists, like Ulrich Beck and Kwame Anthony Appiah,[15] as a universal ethical system: not in its weak sense of cosmopolitanism as a cultured urbanity but in a strong one as a committed morality, a commitment to the primacy of the individual as the significant unit of moral concern transcending necessarily divisive claims of nation or religion. This is not, of course, the place to enter that debate, nor do I want to claim Shakespeare as the proleptic voice of some notion of "Justice without Borders." Cosmopolitanism, however, has long had a political dimension and charge, sometimes seeming to offer a utopian solution to the problem of ethnic, racial, and religious difference.

But it isn't Shakespeare's solution, and, in any case, Shakespeare comes to the problem from the other side, more interested in the limits and fantasies of inclusivity rather than in the primacy of the claims of the individual in the face of its unifying imperatives. There are many places to see this, but think for a moment of *1 Henry IV*, a play almost contemporaneous with *The Merchant of Venice*, both probably written in 1597. King Henry begins with an image of the unitary state, "[a]ll of one nature, of one substance bred" (1.1.11), to be produced in opposition to an alien "other." Through the agency of holy war, the King would construct the national unity he desperately seeks. The nation that "Did lately meet in the intestine shock/ And furious close of civil butchery,/Shall now in mutual, well-beseeming ranks/March all one way" (1.1.12–15). "One nature," "one substance," "one way": but Henry knows this not the case. Walter Blount's arriving "new lighted from his horse,/Stained with the variation of each soil" (1.1.63–4) suggests something of the impossibility of such unity, and, in any case, the King's strategy for producing it cannot be put into action: "But this our purpose now is twelve month old,/And bootless 'tis to tell you we will go" (1.1.28–9).

The reality of new civil broils demands his attention, mocking and making impossible the unifying act he proposes. At the end, however, with the rebels defeated, Henry orders his troops to follow up their advantage and extinguish the remaining pockets of resistance:

> Rebellion in this land shall lose his sway
> Meeting the check of such another day;
> And, since this business so fair is done,
> Let us not leave till all our own be won.
>
> (5.5.41–4)

The homonymic pun between "won" and "one" (inexact but recognizable in late-sixteenth-century London English, as is that between "own" and "one") enacts the political process of unification, aurally reconciling what can only be coerced. Winning is one-ing, we might say (and one-ing is owning, and usually accomplished by winning) but the process of incorporation in the play involves a more violent repression of difference than can comfortably be admitted. In *1 Henry IV,* difference must be overcome by coercion; only what is won is one.[16]

But Venice was a city that embraced difference, perhaps that was even defined by it. It was a living paradox.[17] Contarini celebrates Venice's "wonderful concourse of strange and forraine people,"[18] but recognizes that this makes it even more remarkable that the city "is contained and linked together in a certain vnitie" (sig. F3ʳ). For Contarini, the political miracle is achieved by its form of government, "a temperature," in Lewkenor's English, (that is, a reciprocity or partnership) "between the state of nobility & popular sort" (sig. C3ᵛ), ensuring the whole "doth grow (as it were) into a wel concenting harmony of an excellent commonwealth" (sig. F2ᵛ). But Shakespeare's two Venice plays are not so sanguine. The action of both might be understood as the discovery of the limits of the city's proud cosmopolitanism by its prominent outsiders, their discovery, that is, not only of the flimsiness of that "temperature," which is claimed as the necessary condition of the Republic's "well-concenting harmony," but also how one-sided the arrangement ultimately is.

Let's start by looking at *The Merchant of Venice*. Unquestionably the play is more troubling for us than for Shakespeare and his age, but the surplus is of degree not kind; only the scale of the Holocaust, not its fact, has changed its significance for us. We cannot help but look back at the play through that murderous filter. Our modern history is what overcharges it, but the challenge and the vulnerability of the Jew to the desire for unity is not only a modern problem. Nonetheless, though other plays by Shakespeare have provoked spirited debates about their meaning, no other play has provoked serious questions of whether it should be taught or performed at all.

At best, *The Merchant of Venice* is embarrassing for us; at worst, it is profoundly disturbing. Communities regularly consider whether its members can safely be subjected to it, sometimes succeeding in removing it from classroom syllabi or from the repertory of local theaters, or, less hysterically, surrounding the play with learned discussion in playbills and talkbacks, at least in part apotropaically calculated to relax any possible concern that our educational and cultural institutions have thoughtlessly invited some corrosive poison into their midst. The source of the anxiety is clear enough. It is the worry that the play is anti-Semitic, or could seem so. It is the worry that Shakespeare, whom we celebrate as the voice and guarantor of our best moral and emotional lives, in fact endorses values we have come to find abhorrent or, more worrisome, endorses values that some might *not* find abhorrent.[19]

We have found some predictable ways to ease our anxiety. Often we appeal to the play's manifest subtlety of focus and design. We point, for instance, to the Christian community's inability to live up to its own professed ideals in the play. We observe, too, that if Shylock hates the Christians, his hatred is little different from the Christians' no less reflexive hatred of the Jews. And perhaps we insist that there is more than just an *even* balance. As Hazlitt noted in the nine-teenth century: "our sympathies are much oftener with [Shylock] than with his enemies. He is honest in his vices; they are hypocrites in their virtues."[20] At the very least we have come to insist upon the dignity that the play seemingly allows Shylock, usually by sentimen-tally invoking the speech in which he declares his shared humanity with his Christian antagonists. "Hath not a Jew eyes..." (3.1.53ff) is predictably pointed to as the evidence that Shakespeare neither stigmatizes nor stereotypes Shylock, though inevitably ignoring the speech's actual logic, which extracts, precisely from its assertion of a common humanity, the commitment to hatred and vengeance: "If a Christian wrong a Jew, what should his sufferance be by Christian example? Why, revenge!" (3.1.63–4). Nonetheless, by the late nine-teenth century, especially with the famous performances of Henry Irving, the part became tragic (and an actor's dream), and the play, Shylock's, as it often remains today—the story of a dignified pater-familias, as Irving thought, "almost the only gentleman in the play and the most ill-used."[21]

Or, if we refuse that easy sentimentalizing of the role, we can appeal to history. We can tell ourselves (more or less factually) that there were no Jews—at least no outwardly practicing ones—in Shakespeare's England, the Jewish community having been ban-ished by Edward I in 1290.[22] So, if it looks bad for England, being the first European country formally to expel its Jewish population and willing to welcome them back and allow them to live openly in their faith only about forty years after Shakespeare's death, it may take Shakespeare off the hook.

In the absence of a visible Jewish population, we can tell our-selves that whatever Shakespeare was doing in the play it could not have been intended as an expression of a social prejudice, imagined as any kind of hate-speech directed against a particular group of people, nor could it have provoked others, intentionally or otherwise, to violence against them. There were no real Jews, or at least very few real Jews, and that small number was practic-ing in secret. Jewishness, therefore, can be no more than a meta-phor in the play, a condensation of a set of contrasts with Christian norms: the old law versus the new; the letter versus the spirit; jus-tice versus mercy; getting versus giving—and if these are, as they are, implicitly negative contrasts, they nonetheless function within a purely symbolic economy rather than a social one, and demand to be understood as such. It is worth noting that this is a reading of the play first proposed in 1916, by a Jewish scholar, Sir Israel Gollancz, in a talk to London's Jewish Historical Society.[23]

But even if this is right, that for Shakespeare and his age Jewishness was largely a metaphor, it seems to demand the question of what we should do now, when there are real Jews exposed to the play, and real Jews in the communities in which the play is exposed. Today, Shakespeare's metaphor, a theological anti-Judaism, cannot help but sound like our prejudice, a racial anti-Semitism—but the historical facts may save Shakespeare himself from the charge of being an anti-Semite, at least in any meaningful political sense.

Or, since history at best seems to offer us only a temporary escape, we can appeal to form: the play is a comedy, we can tell ourselves, not about Shylock at all, but a conventional romantic plot that seeks to bring the love of Portia and Bassanio to a happy and harmonious conclusion. Shylock is but a minor character, present in only five of the play's twenty scenes and formally merely a blocking agent, a structural obstacle, for the lovers to overcome, not just Portia and Bassanio, but Jessica and Lorenzo, and even Nerissa and Gratiano. The play begins "with usury and corrupt love; it ends with harmony and perfect love," as Frank Kermode confidently asserts: "And all the time it tells its audience that this is its subject; only by a determined effort to avoid the obvious can one mistake the theme of *The Merchant of Venice*."[24]

But each of these responses seems to me in fact to be far more determined efforts "to avoid the obvious," each an almost perverse attempt to do something that almost any genuine encounter with the play would seemingly make impossible: that is, to tell ourselves that Shakespeare was not fundamentally interested in the unsettling figure of the Jew, and that Shylock should not, in the end, be allowed to disrupt our sense of the play as a comedy or our sense of the city he inhabits as "a well-concenting harmony." Even the titular merchant, we are often told, sometimes needing to be reminded, is not Shylock but Antonio, who hazards all to aid his friend's courtship of Portia.

Perhaps the most considerable objection to allowing Shylock to dominate our sense of the play may be the generic argument. The play is formally a romantic comedy, and our focus upon Shylock—perhaps inevitable in an age in which ethnic identities are so charged and vulnerable—disrupts the play's primary narrative. But perhaps it shouldn't. The comic logic is always that young love will triumph over paternal anxiety; indeed the comic logic more or less demands paternal anxiety as the psychological and formal impediment that must be overcome. Shylock is that impediment, at least the only living one. Portia's father is dead, though his "will" must be done for the comedy to succeed. Shylock, however, as Stephen Orgel has noted, is "that stock figure of Italian comedy the pantaloon":

> Pantalone is the heavy father morbidly protective of his daughter Columbine. Sixteenth- and seventeenth-century visual depictions of him might be depictions of the original Shylock: he is elderly, he has a hooked nose, and he carries a large, wickedly curved knife in his belt. Irascible and vindictive, he is driven wild by his daughter Columbine's flirtations with Harlequin and other young men. Making off with his daughter and his ducats is no more than a condign punishment, and entirely predictable comic conclusion.[25]

However much, then, that we may insist upon the particularity of Shylock's character and situation, a particularity determined by his Judaism, undoubtedly we need to recognize the figure of the pantaloon in his literary past as clearly as the familiar, corrosive, anti-Semitic stereotypes.

Put differently, Shylock is not the disruptive presence that prevents *The Merchant of Venice* from assuredly inhabiting the generic space of comedy, but in fact is part of its defining comic design. Indeed it is arguably the play's other merchant of Venice whose presence actually disrupts the formal structure. Antonio is the odd man out in the multiple couplings that fulfill the emotional impetus of the comedy, even as he stands for the economic energies of the commercial city, which would claim comedy as the rightful acknowledgment of its professed motives and practices.

But in so many ways the comedy is uncomfortable with the ending it formally demands and seemingly offers. "How sweet the moonlight sleeps upon this bank," says Lorenzo to Jessica in one of the play's most lyrical speeches: "Here we will sit and let the sounds of music/Creep in our ears. Soft stillness and the night/Become the touches of sweet harmony" (5.1.54–7). Mustn't we be meant to feel that caress, to enjoy those "touches of sweet harmony"? Certainly this sounds like, and seems designed to produce, uncontaminated romantic enjoyment.

> In such a night as this,
> When the sweet wind did gently kiss the trees
> And they did make no noise, in such a night
> Troilus methinks mounted the Troyan walls,
> And sighed his soul toward the Grecian tents
> Where Cressid lay that night.

(5.1.1–6)

Six similar speeches follow. In each the gentle lyricism of Belmont, with the sweet wind tenderly kissing the trees, contrasts with the stringent legalisms of the Venetian trial scene, even aurally, as the soft sibilants of their verse replace the harsh consonants of the trial in Lorenzo and Jessica's examples of classical lovers who also shared "such a night." But the examples, as we know, can hardly be said to provide comforting precedents: Cressida is taken away from Troilus to marry the Greek Diomedes, becoming a byword for faithlessness; Thisbe (Jessica's answering example) is torn by a lion as she seeks to overcome parental opposition to her love for Pyramis; Dido (Lorenzo's follow-up) kills herself when she is abandoned by Aeneas; Medea (Jessica's counter) kills her children when she thinks herself abandoned by Jason.

Even as jokes these are disturbing ones: stories of betrayal and abandonment, suicide and murder. But at last the lovers turn to themselves:

> In such a night
> Did Jessica steal from the wealthy Jew
> And with an unthrift love did run from Venice
> As far as Belmont.

(5.1.14–17)

> In such a night
> Did young Lorenzo swear he loved her well,
> Stealing her soul with many vows of faith,
> And ne'er a true one.

(5.1.17–20)

Playful, no doubt, the exchange is, but the dark implications are not easily banished by the tone. Perhaps this is all just displacement of their useful knowledge that love involves terrible risks, and the risks can be no better hidden when the lovers shift from their ill-chosen classical analogues to themselves. In the movement from classical mythology to present reality, the threats of betrayal linger: Jessica *steals*, only away from her father, but the syntax ensures that at first we hear the verb differently. We wait for the object and when it does not come we supply it ourselves: she has stolen her father's money and Leah's ring—and Lorenzo has stolen Jessica's soul with vows that may be false.

When Lorenzo focuses Jessica's eye on the physical beauties of the night, the image is revealing: "Look how the floor of heaven/Is thick inlaid with patens of bright gold" (5.1.58–9). Even in Belmont the touches of sweet harmony are unable completely to dissipate the primary Venetian frame of reference. At best they elegantly stylize it; but it inevitably asserts itself, leaving its signature even upon the floor of heaven: "patens of bright gold." "Patens" is the technical term for the gold communion dishes used to hold the consecrated bread, but here the sacramental context gives way to the material.[26] The later Folios even change the unfamiliar word to "patterns"— "patterns of bright gold," editorially performing the spiritual evacuation Lorenzo unconsciously has already achieved. Lorenzo finds the language for what is precious in the golden plates of the communion service rather than in the mystery of the Eucharist itself, that is, in what has a price rather than what is priceless.

The spirit, I suppose we should say, becomes the letter. Critics often note *Shylock's* confusion of categories: "My daughter, my ducats" the most notable, as in his grief he hideously implies their equivalence in his value scheme; or his designation of Antonio as "a good man," meaning only his financial sufficiency rather than any moral excellence. These are regularly pointed to as the signs of his moral limitations. But the world of Venice is no less materially in- terested, only more eloquent in the expression of their shared commitment.

The world of money, commerce, profit, and wealth in this play is not opposed to the world of romantic longing and fulfillment but is revealed as the very condition of it.[27] What, however, is less often observed is that no one in the Christian world would ever deny this. The Christians of the play do not claim the philosophical or moral high ground of anti-materialism. Bassanio's wooing of Portia begins only as the most recent of his "plots and purposes/How to get clear of the debts" he owes (1.1.133–4): "In Belmont is a lady richly left" (1.1.161). This is the observation that begins and motivates the romantic action; and it ends successfully, however stylized, in the same terms, with Portia's "Since you are dear bought, I will love you dear" (3.2.312), revealing how inescapable the economic logic is, its commercial language seemingly inevitable for and fully adequate to the emotional realities it determines and structures.

Christian Venice happily admits its commercial activity. It would, however, insist that its economic principles are morally superior to the corresponding principles of the Jewish world. In part the issue is moneylending.[28] Antonio "lends out money gratis" (1.3.40), responding to the instruction of Luke 6:35 to "lende, looking for nothing againe," while Shylock lends at interest, the Hebrew Bible giving him a wider remit than the good news of Gospel affords: "Vnto a stranger thou maiest lend vpon vsurie, but thou shalt not lende vpon vsurie vnto thy brother" (Deuteronomy 23:20). Shylock's moneylending, then, may well then mark the limits of his own understanding of what it means to be "the Jew of Venyce," although it hardly marks him as unprincipled, or, as the plot makes clear, unneeded.

Obviously, however, both men are equally entrepreneurial and desirous of profit in their commercial activity, but the Christian would achieve it by taking risks, the Jew by risk-free usury.[29] Antonio is a merchant, who would thrive by "venture," to use the play's characteristic word for Venetian commercial activity. Venture is acceptable because there is uncertainty about the outcome; it puts success in the hands of God. Antonio insists that commercial venture is good when it is "A thing not in his power to bring to pass/ But swayed and fashioned by the hand of heaven" (1.3.88–9). Nothing ventured; nothing gained, we might say.[30] Shylock is a merchant, but one who would thrive by usury, to use the loaded term for moneylending. Usury is unacceptable, not merely because of any exorbitant "rate of usance" (1.3.41), which did become the basis of its stigmatization in England.[31] It is figured as unnatural generation: money breeding money, leading Dante to place usurers and sodomites in the same circle of hell. But what seemed most unnatural was the certainty of its profits, the avoidance of God's providence, not just in the money earned from the schedule of interest payments but from the insistence upon collateral that ensures that even if the debt is not repaid the lender cannot lose. "Fast bind; fast find" (2.5.52); so says Shylock. And perhaps it is merely on the basis of those differences in investment strategies that the play world comes to insist that the Jew is the obstacle to harmony and love.

"Which is the merchant here, and which the Jew," asks Portia as she sweeps into the courtroom.[32] It hardly seems a serious question. Could anyone really be uncertain which is which? Isn't this precisely the difference upon which the comedy depends? At the level of the plot, the question is intended to do no more than affirm the reality of the Venetian Portia's disguise as the "young doctor of Rome" (4.1.151–2) in "his" seeming lack of local knowledge. Productions have tended to make the question laughable to an audience, and indeed on stage often the assembled Venetians themselves laugh at the sheer absurdity of it, with Antonio standing in the rich garb of a Venetian nobleman and Shylock dressed in whatever is imagined as his "Jewish gabardine" (1.3.108). How could there be a question? From the first, the scene would visually confirm what it will later verbally assert: the ethical distinction between gentile and Jew, "the difference of *our* spirit" (4.1.364), as the Duke says, gracious and generous, from Shylock's "Jewish heart" (4.1.79), which would get rather than give.

Portia's question, however, echoes through the play. As much as characters assert the radical difference between the merchant and the Jew, the play itself is far less confident that it can be maintained. In various ways, critics have shown how the play collapses the distinction that is insisted upon, and suggests that the Venetians' stigmatization of Shylock is primarily what Leslie Fiedler called "a stratagem for projecting what they must needs recognize as evil in themselves onto an alien Other."[33]

That projection, however, is not just something the play imagines. Christianity itself had long identified the Jew as precisely what the Christian is not: the figure of the Old Testament, of the letter, and of the law, at very best an early and still undeveloped stage of human spirituality, at worst spirituality's malignant opposite. "Paule saith that the Iewes are like to children ... & and we to growen men," wrote Calvin,[34] while Bishop Jewel observed in 1550:

> Chrysostom compareth the state of the Jews unto a candle, and the
> state of the Christians to the brightness of the sun. Again, he likeneth

the Jews to the first draught, or plat of an image, set out only in bare
lines, and the Christians unto the same image lively filled up with all
due proportion, and resemblance and furniture of colours.[35]

Here, in its least noxious form, a supersessional Christianity sees Judaism as some antecedent and inferior form of belief. Christians are
Jews "growen" up, in Calvin's image, or "filled up," in Bishop Jewel's.
Christians complete what Jews only began. This is the revisionary
cultural logic that transforms the Hebrew Bible into the Old Testament, taking the law and its prophets as prefigurations of Christian
revelation. "Thinke not that I am come to destroye the Law or the
Prophetes," says Jesus; "I am not come to destroye them but to fulfil
them" (Matthew 5:17). In this view, as Lisa Freinkel has astutely
noted, "There is, then, no true opposition of Christian and Jew" since
Christianity has been posited "as the true destiny of the Jew."[36]

Too often, however, the opposition is more obviously invidious,
the distinction both mandatory and menacing. The Jew is seen in
this alternative mode not as prototype, not as Jewell's "first draught"
of the Christian waiting to be completed and refined, but as the
Christian's defining antithesis: literal, stubborn, worldly, carnal, de-
generate. Diasporic Jews become "a *whole Nation of Cains*," as John
Donne wrote in a Paul's Cross sermon in May 1627,[37] "*fugitives* and
vagabonds," murderers of the innocent and justly condemned to
wander the earth. The Jew so understood is obviously far less morally redeemable or socially assimilable than the Jew understood as a
Christian prototype. As a credal matter, Jewishness is perhaps not
an intractable social problem, even in an intolerant Christian culture. If Jews are defined by belief, their difference from Christians
may be seen as merely accidental rather than essential, and something that can be overcome. Jews can be saved by conversion, and
only if they refuse to convert, do they merit contempt.

In the play, Jessica's fate confirms this version of Christian universalism; she is unproblematically (if, it should be said, somewhat
tepidly[38]) welcomed into the Christian community. She's the acceptable Jew in the play, though, of course, literally accepted, she ends
up as a Christian. She fulfills the supersessionalist reading of the
instruction of Psalm 45:10 to "forget...thine owne people and thy
father's house." Whatever her Jewishness means it is no barrier to

her assimilation. All she needs to do is abjure her faith and find a Christian to marry. Marriage and apostasy (or is it marriage *as* apostasy) allow the daughter of "a faithless Jew" (2.4.48) to "become a Christian and [Lorenzo's] loving wife" (2.3.21), to become herself "a gentle, and no Jew" (2.6.52), a salutary example of "the unbeleeuing wife," who, according to Paul, can be "sanctified by the husband" (1 Corinthians 7:14).

But Jessica is not the difficult case. First of all, she is a woman, and her body will not bear the mark of God's command to Abraham to "circumcise the foreskin of your flesh" as a "signe of the couenant betwene" God and his chosen people (Genesis 17:11). It unquestionably helps that she is young, she is fair, and perhaps most appealingly (at least to the seemingly unemployed Lorenzo), she comes "furnished" with Shylock's "gold and jewels" (2.4.32). It helps, too, that she is eager to accept her new identity ("ashamed to be [her] father's child," 2.3.17), and that she is enthusiastically invited into it. Shylock is the hard case. He's old, he is unattractive, and he is eager to insist on the same difference that the Christians see between them. "The difference of old Shylock and Bassanio" (2.5.2) is in his mind as telling as the Duke's sense of "the difference of our spirit" from that of the Jew.

In the trial scene, the Duke first appeals to universal values, hoping that Shylock will display the "human gentleness and love" that will release Antonio from the vicious bond. "We all expect a gentle answer," says the Duke (4.1.24, 34). But Shylock, unlike his daughter, is a Jew and no gentle. "[B]y our holy Sabbath have I sworn/To have the due and forfeit of my bond" (4.1.35–6). His "our" is exclusive rather than inclusive, it is the Jews' Sabbath on which he swears, reconfirming his membership in his own "sacred nation" (1.3.44), and thus reversing the valence of Donne's identification of the Jews as "a *whole Nation of Cains*," while in that reversal confirming for many Donne's negative judgment. Shylock's sense of his nation as "sacred" is identical with Donne's sense of its obduracy, and points, in either version, to its immutable separateness.

Father and daughter here figure the two different ways in which Judaism has tended to get boxed in as it is forced to play its ambivalent role in the Christian theological imagination. With no real opportunity to define itself, its options are too often limited to supersession or demonization. And while supersession is obviously the less noxious alternative, and certainly less liable to generate sociopathic responses in extreme situations, it may not get us quite far enough from the anti-Semitism it would try to deny. Judaism may indeed be legitimized by Christianity, as Paul and many later Christian commentators argued, serving as Christianity's authorizing origin, but it is hard to avoid the conclusion that in the process Judaism's own religious status is delegitimized by its successor. This delegitimation starts with the earliest claims of Christian universalism: "there is neither Iewe nor Grecian," as Paul said, "for ye are all one in Christ Iesus" (Galatians 3:28). But another possibility might be a universalism that would not feel the need to deny either the presence or the desirability of Jews and Greeks living *as* Jews and Greeks with all that that entails.

But that is not a possibility that Shakespeare imagines, however much we may wish it were. The comedy indeed depends upon a Christian universalism that remains intact.[39] Jessica can effortlessly enter into the Christian community, proving perhaps that there is no racial animus towards Jews in the play, but pointedly she is welcomed having abandoned her father's faith and bringing with her his ducats. But Shylock cannot be accommodated at all. He is totally absent from the fifth act, and neither mourned nor even remembered except in Lorenzo's one mention of "the Jew" from whom Jessica has stolen.

Shylock's exclusion is the formal acknowledgment of the bitter lesson he learns in the trial about the difference that has everywhere been insisted upon, not least of all by him: the difference between his "our" and their "your." It is "our sacred nation" and "our holy Sabbath" on which he swears, "our synagogue" that he attends (3.1.117), but it is "your charter and your city's freedom" (4.1.38), as he says to the Duke, on which his legal case rests. Acting as a moneylender, Shylock must win his suit, as Antonio knows:

> The Duke cannot deny the course of law;
> For the commodity that strangers have
> With us in Venice, if it be denied
> Will much impeach the justice of the state,
> Since that the trade and profit of the city
> Consisteth of all nations.

> (3.3.26–31)

But once Shylock insists on his bond, on receiving the unprofitable pound of flesh, rather than the "six" thousand ducats Bassanio offers to satisfy the debt (4.1.83), or even six times that amount (4.1.84–5), it becomes clear that his motivations are in no way financial, and do not contribute to "the trade and profit of the city," so what legal protections the city normally offers "strangers" need no longer apply to him. And the law then turns viciously against him, not only in the hyperliteralism of Portia's reading of the contract ("This bond doth give thee here no jot of blood," 4.1.302), but also in the melodramatic revelation that "the law hath yet another hold on" him (4.1.343), a previously unmentioned statute that decrees:

> If it be proven against an alien
> That by direct, or indirect attempts
> He seek the life of any citizen,
> The party 'gainst the which he doth contrive
> Shall seize one-half his goods. The other half
> Comes to the privy coffer of the state
> And the offender's life lies in the mercy
> Of the Duke only, 'gainst all other voice.
>
> (4.1.345–52)

Having been assured by Portia in her role as Balthazar that "the Venetian law/Cannot impugn you as you do proceed" (4.1.174–5), he presses his case only to discover just how seriously the law does impugn him and with what alarming consequences.

If Portia's literal reading of the contract may be said to have a satisfying dramatic and moral logic as a response to Shylock's legalistic instance on the terms of his bond and serves, of course, to save Antonio's life, this hither-to-unmentioned law seems only to confuse the moral and legal issues, or perhaps to make them clear for the first time.[40] It is not necessary in order to save Antonio's life, and seems to be invoked only to be punitive, though, in fairness, perhaps justly so, as Shylock might be guilty of attempted murder. But had he known of the law, he might well never have suggested the original contract or pressed his claim that it be fulfilled.

Or maybe he might have assumed it didn't apply to him. What makes him an alien? Is it merely the fact of being a Jew? And if he is an alien, one might then wonder why the law applies unequally: an alien found guilty of seeking to kill a citizen has his property confiscated and his life is forfeit; but seemingly it is not the other way around (which must be the case or there would be no reason to articulate the law in the terms of citizenship at all). But by holding this law in reserve, Venice gets to present itself as fully cosmopolitan, celebrating and exploiting its liberal republican ideology, all the while aware that "the justice of the state" (3.3.29) ultimately assumes and protects the superior value of its native (or is that Christian?) citizens. A Christian life is worth more than a Jewish one, at least in the sense that an "alien" who seeks a Christian's life is punished more harshly than a Christian seeking an alien's, marking the limits of the city's claim to equality and justice.

Of course, the Duke at the end of the trial will pardon Shylock's life to show "the difference of our spirit," and if the law would confiscate all of Shylock's wealth, half designated for Antonio and half for Venice, even that may be mitigated, although the language is crabbed: "half comes to the general state,/Which humbleness may drive unto a fine" (4.1.367–8). It may sound as if the Duke is saying that instead of taking the half owed the state, he will settle for a "fine." But it is more likely that the full confiscation is itself the "fine" that the Duke in his "humbleness" will take in lieu of taking Shylock's life. But when Portia then asks Antonio, "What mercy can you render him?" (4.1.374), he replies in terms that are more generous:

> So please my lord the Duke and all the court
> To quit the fine for one half of his goods,
> I am content, so he will let me have
> The other half in use, to render it
> Upon his death unto the gentleman
> That lately stole his daughter.
> Two things provided more: that for this favour
> He presently become a Christian;
> The other, that he record a gift
> Here in the court of all he dies possessed
> Unto his son Lorenzo and his daughter.

> (4.1.376–86)

This proposal too is crabbed, but I take it that what he is suggesting is that the Duke give up ("quit") the state's half of Shylock's wealth (or if the Duke's earlier offer is indeed to reduce the state's half to merely a fine, then Antonio asks him to forgive even this), while he will give up his own claim on the rest in order to invest it on behalf of Lorenzo and Jessica, thus leaving Shylock with half, while the other half is "in use" for his daughter and her husband. But then he adds two provisions: 1) that Shylock not be allowed to disinherit his daughter (the "gift...of all dies possessed" to be deeded now "Unto his son Lorenzo and his daughter"); and 2) "He presently become a Christian."

Antonio's "mercy" is, in a way we often forget, indeed merciful: at worst, he may be said to appropriate one half of Shylock's wealth, settle it upon a son-in-law the Jew has every reason to despise, deny him the right to control his inheritance, and insist upon his conversion to Christianity. But we might construe it differently: as allowing Shylock one half of his fortune to continue on with his life, providing for his daughter's and her family's future, and offering the Jew a way to save his soul. And this is, it must be said, mercy that "is not strained." Perhaps it is not exactly mercy that "droppeth as the gentle rain from heaven" (4.1.180–1), but, under the circumstances, it is unexpectedly and remarkably generous. Certainly it is more so than the Duke's offer, and, if one may hear Antonio's "favour" as sarcastic, the proposal is unquestionably free of the venom that marked his earlier dealings with Shylock, spurning and spitting on him, and promising to do it again (1.3.125–6).

On the Rialto, Antonio displays the reflexive contempt for the Jew that, no less than Gratiano's malevolence, undermines the city's self-regard; in the courtroom, however, he enacts a version of the city's imagined magnanimity. And yet it is difficult for us to hear the speech this way.[41] What is usually most unsettling to a modern audience is the proviso "That he presently become a Christian." Antonio's earlier, mocking response to Shylock's offer to provide the money that Bassanio needs, "The Hebrew will turn Christian" (1.3.174), is no longer a patronizing joke but now a stipulated requirement, as the earlier "will" gets transformed in recollection from an auxiliary verb expressing future action to one expressing present necessity.

At the end of the play the Hebrew *will* turn Christian as the condition of the mercy that is offered, and perhaps even as a component of it. Our own commitment to religious toleration, our confidence that there are many mansions in the house of the Lord, makes it hard to credit that this is an act of kindness toward Shylock.[42] And yet it is true that sixteenth-century Christians, like some of their twenty-first century brethren, would believe that only by converting could Shylock be saved. Perhaps Shylock's forced conversion is, if not unambiguously merciful, at least an example of the paradoxical "charitable hatred" Alexandra Walsham has discussed, "a charity towards the sinner that was inextricable from the fervent hatred for the sin that endangered his or her salvation."[43] Theologians of various Christian denominations insisted that to believe in an "irreligious religion," in Purchas's term, was to ensure the death of the soul. Luther wrote that "such blindness must be...compelled and forced by the law to seek something beyond the law and its own ability, namely the grace of God promised in the Christ who was to come."[44] "Compell them to come in," Jesus says (Luke 14:23).

But there is no thought in the play—or even in Luke or Luther—of how such compulsion would work. If conversion needs to be compelled, if, that is, it is to be accomplished against one's will, in what sense is it a conversion, which is a transformation of the will that must be, one might say, willingly accepted? "When any man is converted," wrote William Perkins, "this work of God is not done by compulsion, but he is conuerted willingly: and at the very time when he is conuerted, by Gods grace he wils his co[n]version."[45] Thomas Adams similarly insisted that conversion happens only as God "conuerts our wils to will our owne conuersion."[46]

One might wonder, then, how really "charitable" Antonio's request is; the hatred part, we know. If he understands that conversion cannot in fact save Shylock's soul, then it is only a further effort to humiliate him, and if Antonio thinks it can, then the proviso merely reanimates the universalism that is the origin of the problem. In either case it is not an invitation but a requirement, and one that can only be enforced in outward practice—that is, in ways that cannot possibly matter if it *is* intended to save a soul. Here, then, the "difference" of the Christian spirit that the Duke insists upon seems a lot like the Jewish letter. And by the fifth act, the Jew, of course, is gone. Any fantasy of incorporation is denied by the plot.

In Shakespeare's other Venice play, Othello has indeed turned Christian. He is seemingly a willing convert, though it isn't clear from what, or in what he actually believes. His origins are as obscure as Shylock's,[47] but, unlike Shylock, who is marginal if economically necessary (and would have, although the play ignores the fact, been literally ghettoized in Venice), Othello is central, both formally and culturally. He's the protagonist instead of the pantaloon, a celebrated hero, the city's protector against the "Turk," and he is married, although secretly, to a senator's daughter. Desdemona is able to look past the superficial difference of skin color to see "Othello's visage in his mind" (1.3.253), another point of difference with the comedy. In *The Merchant of Venice*, the Prince of Morocco, understandably worried that the dice are loaded against him in the lottery for Portia's hand, asks her to "Mislike me not for my complexion" (2.1.1–2). Portia offers some slight assurance that "In terms of choice I am not *solely* led/By nice direction of a maiden's eyes" (2.1.13–14, emphasis mine), although when the Prince chooses incorrectly, she sighs with relief, "Let all of his complexion choose me so" (2.7.78–9); and indeed at the beginning of the play, she had already shown her "mislike" when news is brought of the Prince's imminent arrival: "If he have the condition of a saint and the complexion of a devil, I had rather he should shrive me than wive me" (1.2.124–6). Portia never sees the Prince's visage in her mind, only in her eye—through the filter of the color of his skin.

Or maybe it's not the issue of race per se for Portia but the association of skin color with religion.[48] Venice hasn't proven itself exactly a hotbed of respectful interfaith dialogue. Black equals Moor equals Muslim. It was thought that North African pagans had been converted to Islam. Johan Boemus reported that many formerly pagan Africans were now "worshippers of Mahomet…and are called Maures, or Moores,"[49] although it must be said there is nothing in the play that marks Othello as having been one. But in *Othello* Desdemona gets some help in seeing Othello's visage in his mind, because whatever he was, he is now a Christian. Even the furious Brabantio will claim that, in eloping with Othello, Desdemona has offended only against "clime, complexion, and degree," seemingly accepting their common religion, though their shared faith will not save them, at least in this world. In this world, of course, a different kind of faith would be required to turn the tragedy into comedy. "My life upon her faith," (1.3.295), says Othello, although the play's tragic truth is that it is exactly the reverse.[50]

Iago, too, admits Othello's Christianity, noting his "baptism,/All seals and symbols of redeemed sin" (2.3.338–9), as the index of what is most important to Othello, but which he will risk for Desdemona: "His soul is so enfettered to her love." In this play, then, religion is not the central social problem; race is—though at least in part this is so because religion gets ameliorated as a problem precisely because of race. *Othello* relaxes the anxiety about conversion precisely because it keeps visible the difference that Jewish conversion would efface, especially since Judaism's telltale mark of difference, circumcision, is invisible to all but the most intimate observers and, of course, a defining sign only for males. The true sign of Jewish otherness is inside—a difference of spirit, as the Christian world in *The Merchant of Venice* anxiously insists—hence the need at times to make Jews wear some badge outside to confirm it.[51]

But the badge of racial difference is racial difference itself. The prophet Jeremiah asks, "Can the blacke More change his skin, or the leopard his spots?" (Jeremiah 13:23), in his warning to the Hebrew people against becoming accustomed to sin, and the proverbial phrases for impossibility echo through early modern England. Elnathan Parr, a Suffolk minister, insisted: "If thou be truly conuerted, ascribe al the glory of it to God: for as soone can an Ethiop change his skinne, or a Leopard his spottes, as we doe that is good, till we be changed and enabled by the Spirit."[52] The things that are impossible with men are possible with God (Luke 18:27), and, thus, Richard Crashaw, in his poem "On the Baptized Aethiopian," deploys the proverbial claim only to deny its truth: "Let it no longer be a forlorn hope/To wash an Ethiope," says Crashaw, because the acceptance of Christ will turn the Ethiope's soul "white," and the "Eternal Dove" will then love its "black-fac'd house."

Othello is similar to Crashaw's "Baptized Ethiope." There's no doubt the play insists upon his blackness. He isn't Everyman. He's referred to as "the thick lips" (1.1.66) and "an old black ram" (1.1.88) with "a sooty bosom" (1.2.70). Blackness is so central even to his own self-image and imagining that when he tries to find terms to measure the change in his understanding of Desdemona's moral being, the best he can come up with is: "Her name, that was as fresh/As Dian's visage, is now begrimed and black/As mine own face" (3.3.389–91).

It is, however, worth remembering that in Shakespeare's theater you *could* wash an Ethiope white—indeed it could not be otherwise, with no black actors to take the role.[53] A white actor had to "black up" to play it, and would be washed back to his natural skin color once the performance ended. It is hard to know how much an early modern audience while watching *Othello* would register this fact (any more than we can know the effect of boy actors playing women on the cultural understanding of gender difference). It is hard to know, that is, how much the Duke's attempt to reassure Brabantio, "Your son-in-law is far more fair than black" (1.3.291), might be heard as a metatheatrical joke rather than as the expression of the same Christian universalism that Crashaw voices, though even as metadrama it would reinforce the stubborn reality of actual racial difference.

Othello can convert, but the Ethiope, or whatever nationality he is by birth (perhaps Mauritanian[54]), cannot be washed white, and, even if his soul *is* so washed, its "black faced house" is likely to be more unequivocally loved by the Holy Spirit than by the citizens of Venice. There is at least a hint of this in the play, perhaps in the Duke's unmotivated question about the whereabouts of the mysterious Marcus Luccicos once the Turkish threat is announced (1.3.45)[55] and no doubt in the speed with which "they do command [Othello] home/Deputing Cassio in his government" (4.1.235–6) once the Turkish fleet is lost in a storm. Othello is embraced when he is needed either to lead an army against the Turks or, in times of peace, to serve as a dinner guest, but he can never be fully naturalized. He is a Moor, he is *the* Moor, an identification even turned into a mocking term of office: "his Moorship," as Iago calls him (1.1.32). And that fact makes him inevitably suspect, despite his conversion—or even because of it. "*Marrani*," was the word, as Edwin Sandys defined it, for "baptized *Iews* or *Moors*," who converted only to escape prosecution and who remained "utterly adverse" to the Christian religion.[56]

In early modern England, "Moor," far more than "Jew," was a radically unstable signifier, an ethnographic catchall, as Michael Neill has demonstrated.[57] It might be a geographic, racial, or a religious category, referring to the Berber-Arabs of a geographically capacious Morocco, to dark-skinned Africans in general, to Ottoman

Turks, or to Muslims in general, often blurring or collapsing the different meanings. But the play tries to stabilize the term—or at least Othello does. Iago energetically exploits the instability to provoke a range of stereotypical associations all involving uncontrolled or uncontrollable passions, but Othello wants to ensure that it refers only to his origin and his outside, neither to be denied but neither sufficient to prevent his acceptance into Venetian society. The man Rodrigo would see as "an extravagant and wheeling stranger" (1.1.134)[58] surrounds himself and is surrounded by adjectives of both stability and well-being. He is a "full soldier" (2.1.36), of "solid virtue" (4.1.266) and with a "perfect soul" (1.2.31).

Othello is seemingly at ease with himself as a Christian Moor, a naturalized European, having self-fashioned an identity that is "all in all sufficient" (4.1.265), so much so that he can accusingly ask the brawling Venetians in 2.3, "Are we turned Turks?" (166), assuming his inclusion and accepting the risk of being charged, we might say, with being the pot that calls the kettle black. He confidently asserts his own difference from the dark Islamic outsiders, who serve as the marker here of wildness and violence in opposition to the standard of Venetian decorum that he will in various senses uphold.[59]

"To turn Turk," was, of course, more specifically to abjure Christianity and convert to Islam,[60] and Othello's use of the familiar phrase, even as a mere term of derogation, no doubt speaks to his own confidence in his cultural position, achieved only through his own turning. But the full sentence, no less derogatory about the violent disorderliness of the evening, perhaps betrays the strain of maintaining it. "Are we turned Turks and to ourselves do that/ Which Heaven hath forbid the Ottomites?" (2.3.166–7). What "Heaven hath forbid the Ottomites," according to Graham Holderness, "is alcohol, so the issue here is that drunken Christians show to distinct disadvantage by contrast with sober and religious Muslims."[61] Certainly Cassio regrets his drunkenness: "O God, that men should put an enemy in their mouths, to steal away their brains" (2.3.285–6), and his behavior is both unbecoming and inappropriate in the anxious fortress town.

But what is also forbidden the Turks is to fight among themselves. Richard Knolles in his *General History of the Turks*, published in 1603, writes of the Turks that "they call themselues *Islami*, that is to say, men of one mind, or, at peace among themselves."[62] But the two clauses of Othello's question are then difficult to bring together into a single thought. If the question means, as it might be glossed, "do we fight amongst ourselves, which [even] the Turks are forbidden to do by their religion,"[63] then "turned Turks" is a curiously inept metaphor, arguably the worst possible one, and producing complete contradiction: we are like the Turks in doing what Turks are forbidden to do.

What I think Othello actually means is that in their violence the brawling Venetians have "turned Turk," but haven't turned quite Turk enough, because fully converted Turks would not be fighting each other. Turks did, of course, fight, and early modern European observers attributed their remarkable expansionist success to the fact that, as Fynes Moryson says, their "lawe teacheth to ioyne in brotherly loue, and to vent all their anger and rage vppon the Common Enemyes of their Country and the Lawes of Mahomett."[64] Is "Turk," then, a term of contempt or praise? The answer is not so obvious. There is admiration and envy, and there is fear and condescension. Othello's sentence breaks logically at the point that fear of Turkish military power gives way to admiration of their unity—to admiration, that is, of what exactly a fractured post-Reformation Europe lacked. Knolles's *Generall Historie of the Turks* recognizes as one of the major causes of "the Turks greatnesse" the "rare vnitie and agreement amongst them…in the manner of their religion," which is immediately denigrated with a parenthetical "(if it be so to be called)," and the large *Historie* is designed in large part to urge King James to join forces with the other Christian princes of Europe, for "onely by your vnited forces (the barbarous enemies greatest terror)" can the Turkish threat be defeated (sig. A3ᵛ).

But for Othello the sentence is more psychologically revealing than politically. It exposes a fault line in the identity he has so carefully constructed, raising questions both about what he has turned to and turned against, not least as a result of the oddity of "Heaven" giving the Turks such good advice. Othello is caught between cultural positions. The very claim that he is a "noble moor" (2.3.134; 3.4.26; 4.1.264), three times repeated, begins to sound like an oxymoron (all too much like the "gentle Jew" in *Merchant of Venice*, 1.3.73), and indeed the play is the agonizing history of Othello's inability by force of will to make some "concord of this discord," as a different play puts it (*A Midsummer Night's Dream* 5.1.60), or to participate in the "well-concenting harmony" that Venice imagines as its own. If the Jew who will not convert is an "alien" in Venice, so too is the Moor who will: a faithless Jew and a "base Judean" (5.2.345), at least as the Folio has it.[65]

If Venice is a paradox, Othello is a paradox within that paradox, as he himself agonizingly will discover:

> in Aleppo once,
> Where a malignant and a turbaned Turk
> Beat a Venetian and traduced the state,
> I took by th' throat the circumcised dog,
> And smote him—thus.

> (5.2.350–4)

Anagnorisis and catastrophe are here one. He is both the "malignant" Turk and the Christian champion, his act completing his terrible journey to destruction but also marking a return to his former dignity.[66] He, not Desdemona, will "turn, and turn, and yet go on,/And turn again" (4.1.277–8)—turn Christian, turn Turk, and turn once more to try to reconcile the contradiction. And the scene he invokes is carefully located. Aleppo, in Northern Syria, played much the same role in the Ottoman Empire as Venice did in Christian Europe and thus is the perfect setting for Othello's ambivalent action. It was a cosmopolitan trading center at its edge, though looking West instead of East, and in fact, as Hakluyt notes, a city "wherein continually are many Venetians dwelling."[67] It was a city to which, as John Cartwright says, "resort *Iewes, Tartarians, Persians, Armenians, Egyptians, Indians*, & many sorts of Christians, all enioying freedome of conscience,"[68] and a city "of wonderful great trading," as Robert Coverte said in 1612, "as well knowne to England (or at least to our English Merchants) as Kingstone upon Thames"[69] (sig. I3ᵛ) —though the shopping in Aleppo was no doubt better. What Othello recalls is not his exotic African past, as he does in his tale that won Brabantio's daughter, but his European present. In the suicidal act he becomes for one last time the defender of Venice and the Christian West, as he was meant to be when he was sent to Cyprus,[70] again executing justice on "malignant and a turbaned Turk" who has "Beat a Venetian and traduced the state."

Othello enacts the paradox that he knows himself to be. He knows he cannot be fully naturalized: he cannot be made one with the culture or even one with himself. He is, as the quarto title page says, "The Moore of Venice," but by the end of the play it is clear this phrase is incapable of denoting some well-integrated social identity but can only point at an impossibly divided self. Brabantio speaks the essentializing social logic determining Othello's difference in his certainty that Othello could only have won Desdemona with witchcraft: "For nature so preposterously to err" (1.3.63). But Othello will himself ultimately agree. "And yet how nature erring against itself" (3.3.231), he begins, as his belief both in Desdemona's honesty and his own worth crumbles. Iago jumps in right there, recognizing that what Othello so obviously has internalized will provide the means to undo him: "Ay, there's the point" (3.3.232). The very line that seems to mark Q1 *Hamlet* as a "bad" quarto ("To be or not be, I there's the point," sig. D4^v) is in *Othello* the line that marks the tragic tipping "point" in Othello's harrowing disintegration from him who was "once so good" (5.2.288). It's the line that makes the "point" about the insufficiency of the identity Othello has framed for himself, and it's the line that brings us to the "point" at which Venice, in its conventional understanding of what is natural, reveals itself as so much less cosmopolitan than it imagines itself to be— with devastating implications both for the Jew who underwrites its economic system and for the Moor who protects the city.[71]

But if not Venice, then where? Certainly not in Shakespeare's England, where Jews would not be readmitted and allowed to live openly as Jews for another half century, and also where, in 1601, "Negroes and blackamoors" were ordered to be deported because of the inconvenience of their growing numbers, not least as a result of the fact that "the most of them are infidels having no understanding of Christ or his Gospel."[72]

But also not in Shakespeare's plays. We can read *The Merchant of Venice* and *Othello* as critiques of Venetian self-regard, even of the inadequacies of Christian universalism to resolve the problems of difference, but Shakespeare himself too readily reproduces the familiar discourse of privilege and centrality to let him serve as the prophetic voice of universal fellowship. In *Macbeth*, a "Liver of blaspheming Jew" (4.1.26) is added to the witches' cauldron, but of course this is an ingredient in a witch's recipe. More unsettling are the careless, perfunctory usages. "I am a Jew else, an 'Ebrew Jew," says Falstaff (*1 Henry IV*, 2.4.173) as a validation of the truth of what he has just spoken, and Benedick will define his commitment to Beatrice similarly: "if I do not love her I am a Jew" (*Much Ado About Nothing*, 2.3.253). It is the sheer conventionality of the usage of "Jew" as a synonym for a "liar" or "betrayer" that is disturbing, precisely from the fact that it is not intended as an insult at all.

Turks fare little better. Their body parts also find their place in the witches' stew ("Nose of Turk, and Tartar's lips," 4.1.29), and similarly their name becomes a conventional term of contempt. In *Merry Wives*, Pistol calls Falstaff a "[b]ase Phrygian Turk" (1.3.85), outraged by Falstaff's arrogance and ambition. And Moors are "barbarous" and "irreligious," though those are the terms the Roman world of *Titus Andronicus* (5.3.4,120) uses ineffectively to distinguish the actions of "Aaron the Moor" from its own behavior. Shakespeare indeed succeeds in giving both Shylock and Othello a complex psychology that makes each more than a stereotype. He differentiates Shylock from the Jew of medieval blood libels and from Marlowe's Barabas, and Othello from the Africans of traveler's accounts "in olde tyme called *Ethiopes* and *Nigrite*, which we now call Moores, Moorens, or *Negros*, a people of beastly lyuyng, without a God, lawe, religion,"[73] and from the predictable villainies of Aaron. Nonetheless, Shakespeare fails to imagine worlds in which even three-dimensional Jews and Moors can avoid the bitter discovery of how provisional and vulnerable their existence is within the universalist fantasies of both Christian theology and Venetian commercial ideology. But, of course, he never set out to do so.

Notes

1 Eliade, *The Sacred and the Profane*, trans. Willard R. Trask (1957; New York: Harcourt, 1968), 62. For a valuable account of the history of the word "religion," see Wilfred Cantwell Smith, *The Meaning and End of Religion* (1962; New York: Fortress Press, 1991), 19ff; see also Talal Asad, *Genealogies of Religion: Discipline and Reasons of Power in Christianity and Islam* (Baltimore, MD: Johns Hopkins University Press, 1993).

2 Among the many accounts of the historical development of an understanding of religion as a sphere of private belief distinct from the world

of secular activity and authority, see Timothy Fitzgerald, "Encompassing Religion, privatized religions, and the invention of modern politics," in *Religion and the Secular: Historical and Colonial Formations*, ed. Timothy Fitzgerald (London: Equinox, 2007), 211–40.

3 See, for example, Peter Harrison, *"Religion" and the Religions in the English Enlightenment* (Cambridge: Cambridge University Press, 1990); and Jonathan Z. Smith, "Religion, Religions, Religious," in *Critical Terms for Religious Studies*, ed. Mark C. Taylor (Chicago, IL: University of Chicago Press, 1998), 269–84.

4 Alfield, *A true reporte of the death & martyrdome of M. Campion Iesuite and preiste, & M. Sherwin, & M. Bryan preistes* (London, 1582), sig. B1ʳ.

5 John Taylor, *The Anatomy of the Separatists* (London, 1642), sig. A2ʳ.

6 Brereward, *Enquiries Touching the Diversity of Languages and Religions through the Chiefe Parts of the World* (London, 1614), sig. L3ᵛ.

7 Bossy, "Some Elementary Forms of Durkheim," *Past and Present* 95 (1982), 6.

8 Bate, *The Portaiture of Hypocrisie* (London, 1589), sig. G3ᵛ.

9 Samuel Purchas, *Purchas His Pilgrimage* (London, 1614), sig. D4ᵛ.

10 Jefferson, *Notes on the State of Virginia* (London, 1787), 267, 265.

11 Emerson, "Shakespeare; or, The Poet," *Representative Men in Essays and Lectures*, ed. Joel Porte (New York: Library of America, 1983), 721.

12 Benjamin Disraeli, *Tancred, or the New Crusade* (London: Henry Colborn, 1847), 299.

13 I am using "cosmopolitan" here in a sense derived from the modern social sciences to define a political entity that recognizes the rights of individuals without privileging considerations of nationality, ethnicity, or religion. Forms of the word ("cosmopolitic" and "cosmopolitical") are commonly used in early modern English, usually, however, to refer to individuals without strong "national attachments or prejudices" (*OED*), though there are usages uncited in the *OED* where it means something very much like this modern sense. William Barlow, for example, can imagine a "Cosmopoliticall vnion of humane societie," in his *The Navigators Supplie* (London, 1597), sig. b.2ʳ.

14 Coryate, *Coryats Crudities* (London, 1611), sig. O7ᵛ.

15 See Beck's *Cosmopolitan Vision*, trans. Ciaran Cronin (Malden, MA: Polity Press, 2006); and Appiah's *Cosmopolitanism: Ethics in a World of Strangers* (New York: W. W. Norton, 2006).

16 For a fuller account of this process, see my "'The King Hath Many Marching in his Coats,' or, What Did You Do in the War, Daddy?," in *Shakespeare after Theory* (London and New York: Routledge, 1999), 129–47.

17 See Peter G. Platt, *Shakespeare and the Culture of Paradox* (Farnham, Surrey, and Burlington, VT: Ashgate, 2009), 57–94; Nick Potter, in *Shakespeare: The Play of History*, eds. Graham Holderness, Nick Potter, and John Turner (Iowa City: University of Iowa Press, 1987), calls Venice an

"oxymoron" (p. 193); and John Gillies, in *Shakespeare and the Geography of Difference* (Cambridge: Cambridge University Press, 1994), calls the city "a glorious—yet unsettling—contradiction" (p. 123).

18 Gasparo Contarini, *Commonwealth and Gouernment of Venice*, trans. Lewis Lewkenor (London, 1599), sig. B1^r.

19 Of course, there are other plays that might suggest the distance between our culture and Shakespeare's, complicating our conviction that Shakespeare was "not of an age." *The Taming of the Shrew*, as Claire McEachern reminds me, produces a similar concern that Shakespeare might be thought to endorse female submission to patriarchy, but less cultural anxiety surrounds this possibility, maybe suggesting that we find it less offensive to coerce women than Jews.

20 William Hazlitt, "Kean's Debut as Shylock, 1816," in *The Merchant of Venice*, eds. William Baker and Brian Vickers (London and New York: Continuum, 2005), 31.

21 Quoted in Jeffrey Richards, *Sir Henry Irving: A Victorian Actor and His World* (New York: Continuum, 2005), 427.

22 See James Shapiro's indispensible *Shakespeare and the Jews* (New York: Columbia University Press, 1996), 55–76.

23 It may have been Lawrence Danson who first noted the irony of this fact; see his decidedly unironic *The Harmonies of "The Merchant of Venice"* (New Haven, CT: Yale University Press, 1978), 14; see also Shapiro, 77–80. Gollancz's lecture, "The 'Shylock' of Shakespeare," was published in *Allegory and Mysticism in Shakespeare: A Medievalist on "The Merchant of Venice": Reports of Three Lectures by Sir Israel Gollancz* (London: Geo. W. Jones, 1931). Probably the most influential modern "allegorical" reading of the play has been Barbara Lewalski's "Biblical Allusion and Allegory in *The Merchant of Venice*," *Shakespeare Quarterly* 13 (1962), 327–43, though many have followed in Lewalski's wake. Lisa Freinkel's *Reading Shakespeare's Will: The Theology of Figure from Augustine to the Sonnets* (New York: Columbia University Press, 2002) provides an extraordinary account of the literary and critical consequences of Christian allegorical norms.

24 Kermode, "Mature Comedies," *Renaissance Essays: Shakespeare, Spenser, Donne* (London: Routledge & Kegan Paul, 1971), 215.

25 Orgel, "Shylock's Tribe," in *Imagining Shakespeare* (Basingstoke, and New York: Palgrave Macmillan, 2003), 156.

26 See Freinkel, *Reading Shakespeare's Will*, 283–4.

27 This has become the central insight of modern ironic readings of the play; see, for example, Eric S. Mallin's observation that even at the level of plot "the Jew works as an integral part of the Christian community by providing the necessary economic conditions for romance," in his trenchant and ludic "Jewish Invader and the Soul of the State: *The Merchant of Venice* and Science Fiction Movies," in *Shakespeare and Modernity:*

Early Modern to Millennium, ed. Hugh Grady (London and New York: Routledge, 2000), 146.

28 John Drakakis's introduction to his Arden edition of the play (London: A & C Black, 2010) includes a useful summary of contemporary attitudes towards usury; see esp. pp. 8–17. See also Norman L. Jones's *God and the Moneylenders: Usury and Law in Early Modern England* (Oxford: Blackwell, 1989).

29 See, for example, Neil Carson, "Hazarding and Cozening in *The Merchant of Venice*," *English Language Notes* 9 (1972), 168–77.

30 Whatever his commitment to an ethic of venture, Antonio seems himself prudently to limit his exposure: "My ventures are not in one bottom trusted" (1.1.41).

31 In 1571, the Act against Usury held that no loan could be "reserved at or taken above the rate of ten pounds for the hundred for one year." Quoted in *A Collection of Statutes Connected with the Administration of the Law*, eds. William David Evans, et al. (London: Thomas Blenkarn, 1836), vol. 2, 284.

32 Among the many critics who have focused on this extraordinary question are Richard Henze, "'Which is the Merchant Here? And Which the Jew?'" *Criticism* 16 (1974), 287–300; Thomas Moisan, "'Which is the merchant here? And which the Jew?': Subversion and Recuperation in *The Merchant of Venice*," in *Shakespeare Reproduced: The Text in History and Ideology*, eds. Jean E. Howard and Marion F. O'Connor (New York and London: Methuen, 1987), 188–206; James Shapiro, "'Which is *The Merchant* here, and Which *The Jew*?': Shakespeare and the Economics of Influence," *Shakespeare Studies* 20 (1988), 269–79; Avraham Oz, "'Which is the Merchant Here? And which the Jew?': Riddles of Identity in *The Merchant of Venice*," in *Shakespeare and Cultural Traditions*, eds. Tetsuo Kishi, Roger Pringle, and Stanley Wells (Newark: University of Delaware Press, 1994), 155–73; Richard Halpern's chapter on the play in his *Shakespeare among the Moderns* (Ithaca: Cornell University Press, 1997), 159–226; and David Nirenberg, "Shakespeare's Jewish Questions," *Renaissance Drama* 38 (2010), 77–113.

33 Fiedler, *Fiedler on the Roof: Essays on Literature and Jewish Identity* (Boston: David R. Godine, 1991), 28.

34 *An Abridgement of the Institution of Christian Religion*, trans. Chistopher Fethertsone (London, 1585), sig. X3^r.

35 Jewel, *A Reply to Mr. Harding's Answer, The Works of John Jewel, Bishop of Salisbury* (Cambridge: Parker Society, 1847), vol. 24, 615.

36 Freinkel, *Reading Shakespeare's Will*, 238.

37 Donne, *Fifty Sermons* (London, 1649), sig. Ii6^r.

38 Except to Lorenzo, Jessica is almost invisible in Belmont, hardly spoken to by anyone, which is only one of Janet Adelman's wonderful observations about Jessica's role in the play; see Adelman, *Blood Relations:*

Christian and Jew in The Merchant of Venice (Chicago, IL: University of Chicago Press, 2008), esp. 66–98.

39 Perhaps the most subtle and also sanguine account of this is Julia Reinhard Lupton's fine chapter on the play in her *Citizen-Saints: Shakespeare and Political Theology* (Chicago, IL: University of Chicago Press, 2005), 73–102, which sees Shylock finally having been "drawn not only back into the circle of humanity, but also toward the circle of Venetian citizenship itself" (p. 99). Lupton provocatively draws upon the revision of Pauline theology by critical theorists like Giorgi Agamben and Alain Badiou. Though not concerned with Shakespeare, see also Gregory Kneidel, *Rethinking the Turn to Religion in Early Modern English Literature: The Poetics of All Believers* (Basingstoke: Palgrave Macmillan, 2008).

40 Avraham Oz calls this "a special anti-terrorist act"; see his "Dobbin on the Rialto: Venice and the Division of Identity," in *Shakespeare's Italy: Functions of Italian Locations in Renaissance Drama*, eds. Michele Marrapodi, A. J. Hoenselaars, Marcello Cappuzzo, and L. Falzon Santucci (Manchester and New York: Manchester University Press, 1993), 196. See also Eric S. Mallin's alert discussion of the belated introduction of this law, in his "Jewish Invader and the Soul of the State: *The Merchant of Venice* and Science Fiction Movies," 154–6.

41 See Harry Berger's "Mercifixion in *The Merchant of Venice*: The Riches of Embarrassment," *Renaissance Drama* 38 (2010): esp. 35–7; A. D. Nutall had earlier sensed "a faint smell of patronizing contempt in the very exercise of mercy." See his *A New Mimesis: Shakespeare and the Representation of Reality* (London and New York: Methuen, 1983), 130.

42 Hugh Short is one of the few recent critics to argue that Antonio's proviso is well-intentioned, "opening up the possibility of salvation to Shylock," and that "Shylock speaks the truth when he says he is content." See his "Shylock is Content: A Study in Salvation," in *The Merchant of Venice: New Critical Essays*, eds. John W. Mahon and Ellen Macleod Mahon (New York and London: Routledge, 2002), 199–212. The quoted phrases are on pages 210 and 202.

43 See Walsham, *Charitable Hatred: Tolerance and Intolerance in England, 1500–1700* (Manchester: Manchester University Press, 2006), 2.

44 Luther, "Preface to the Old Testament," in *Luther's Works: Word and Sacrament*, ed. E. Theodore Bachmann (St Louis, MO: Concordia, 1960), vol. 35, 44.

45 Perkins, *A reformed Catholike, or, A declaration shewing how neere we may come to the present Church of Rome in sundrie points of religion* (London, 1597), sig. A8^r.

46 Adams, *A Diuine Herball together with a Forest of Thornes* (London, 1616), sig. H3^r.

47 See fn. 54.

48 Indeed for Ania Loomba, the central achievement of *Othello* "is that it brings blackness and religious difference into simultaneous play while

also making visible the tensions between them." See her *Shakespeare, Race, and Colonialism* (Oxford: Oxford University Press, 2002), 107.

49 Boemus, *The Fardle of Façions*, trans. William Watreman (London, 1555) sig. C6ᵛ.

50 See Robert N. Watson, "*Othello* as Protestant Propaganda," in *Religion and Culture in Renaissance England*, eds. Claire McEachern and Debora Shuger (Cambridge: Cambridge University Press, 1997), 234–57, who argues that the play transposes ideas about salvation into "the realm of marriage" (p. 234).

51 Fynes Moryson noted that in Prague "The lawe byndes the men to weare red hatts or bonnetts, and the wemen a garment of the same Coller, neere blood, to witnesse their guiltiness of Christs blood," and that "in all places the Jewes long seruitude and wonderfull scattering is exposed to all Christians for a fearefull spectikle, and to themselues for a dayly remembrance of Gods Curse layd vpon them." See *Shakespeare's Europe: Unpublished Chapters of Fynes Moryson's Itinerary*, ed. Charles Hughes (London: Sterratt and Hughes, 1903), 489–90.

52 Parr, *The Grounds of Diuinitie* (London, 1614), sig. P1ᵛ.

53 See Dympna Callaghan, "Othello Was a White Man: Properties of Race on Shakespeare's Stage," *Alternative Shakespeares: Volume 2*, ed. Terence Hawkes (London and New York: Routledge, 1996), 192–215; and also Karen Newman, "'And Wash the Ethiope White,'" in *Shakespeare Reproduced: The Text in History and Ideology*, eds. Jean E. Howard and Marion O'Conner (London: Methuen, 1987), 141–62.

54 See 4.2.226, where Iago tells Roderigo that Othello "goes into Mauretania and taketh away with him the fair Desdemona," perhaps a hint of the origins we are never told of, as Shylock's might be pointed at his own in his reference to the diamond he bought "in Frankfurt" (3.1.76–7).

55 Perhaps a suggestion that he is the Duke's preferred choice for General?

56 Sandys, *Europae speculum, Or, a View or Survey of the State of Religion in the Westerne parts of the World* (London: 1629), sig. X2ᵛ. Florio in his *Worlde of Wordes* (London, 1598) defines *Marano* as "A Iew, an Infidell, a renegado, a nickname for a Spaniard."

57 See Neill's introduction to his excellent edition of *Othello* (Oxford: Oxford University Press, 2006), 115–16. Emily Bartels, in her *Speaking of the Moor: From Alacazar to Othello* (Philadelphia, PA: University of Pennsylvania Press, 2008), comments that "the Moor is first and foremost a figure of uncodified and uncodifiable diversity" (p. 5); and Nabil Matar and Rudolph Stoekel note that "Shakespeare's 'Moors' are an ill-defined group from the bottom third of 'the three-nooked world,'" in "Europe's Mediterranean Frontier: The Moor," in *Shakespeare and Renaissance Europe*, eds. Andrew Hadfield and Paul Hammond (London: Thomson, 2005), 220.

58 This is a phrase that appears among eighteen lines in Roderigo's speech that exist only in the Folio text.

59 It is worth remembering that Shakespeare introduces the Turks into the Othello story; they do not appear in Cinthio's tale in *Hecatommithi*, which serves as Shakespeare's source. There Othello is sent to Cyprus "as Commandant of the soldiers," but there is no mention of a Turkish threat. See *Narrative and Dramatic Sources of Shakespeare*, ed. Geoffrey Bullough (London: Routledge & Kegan Paul, 1973), vol. 7, 239–52.

60 See Daniel Vitkus's important essay, "Turning Turk in Othello: The Conversion and Damnation of the Moor," *Shakespeare Quarterly* 48 (1997), 145–76; and also Jonathan Burton, *Traffic and Turning: Islam and English Drama, 1579–1624* (Newark, DE: University of Delaware Press, 2005), esp. ch. 6.

61 Holderness, *Shakespeare and Venice* (Farnham, Surrey and Burlington, VT: Ashgate, 2010), 104.

62 Knolles, *The Generall Historie of the Turks* (London, 1603), sig. A5^r. For an important account of the significance of Knolles's *Historie*, see Richmond Barbour, *Before Orientalism: London's Theatre of the East, 1576–1626* (Cambridge: Cambridge University Press, 2003), 13–36; and Benedict S. Robinson, *Islam and Early Modern English Literature: The Politics of Romance from Spenser to Milton* (Basingstoke: Palgrave Macmillan, 2007), 71–82.

63 *Othello*, ed. E. A. J. Honigmann (London: Thomson, 1997), Longer Note, p. 337.

64 Moryson, *Shakespeare's Europe: Unpublished Chapters of Fynes Moryson's Itinerary*, 44.

65 The famous crux has been often discussed: Othello sees himself like a base Judean or, in the 1622 Quarto, a "base Indian," throwing "a pearl away/Richer than all his tribe" (5.2.345–6). If he imagines himself as a "base Indian," he imagines himself as innocent and unsophisticated, discarding the pearl unaware of its value, as the Indians of the new world were often described. But the Folio's self-recrimination is sharper; there he imagines his deed as a radical act of betrayal: he becomes Judas (often thought to be the only apostle who was a Judean) betraying the "pearl of great price" that is Christ. It is, however, impossible to tell which word Shakespeare intended. The change could be the result of revision, but we cannot tell which text revises which. The order in which the texts were published tells us nothing about the order in which they were composed, and both were published after Shakespeare was dead. Or maybe it is a variant with no intended semantic distinction. In the Folio, "Judean" is spelled with an "I," so the only significant typographic distinction upon which so much rests is the "u" of "Iudean" and the "n" of "Indian." The variant could then rest on a mere compositorial mistake with a not uncommonly turned "u" or "n," though it is impossible to know which is the erroneously turned piece of type, since we do not know what the manuscript read from which either text was printed; and, in any case, "u" and "n" in the handwriting of the period are themselves often indistinguishable. Bibliographic analysis can't solve this one.

66 See Peter Stallybrass, "Marginal England: The View from Aleppo," in *Center or Margin: Revisions of the English Renaissance in Honor of Leeds Barroll,* ed. Lena Cowen Orlin (Selinsgrove, PA: Susquehanna University Press, 2006), 27–39; see also my *Shakespeare and the Shapes of Time* (London: Macmillan, 1982), esp. 81–2, from which some sentences have been adapted here.

67 Hakluyt, sig. Gg6ʳ.

68 Cartwright, *The Preachers Travels* (London, 1611), sig. B4ᵛ.

69 Coverte, *A True and Almost Incredible Report of an Englishman* (London, 1612), sig. I3ᵛ. Sadly, Aleppo has recently again become "well knowne to England," though not as a cosmopolitan trading center but as the site of unnatural killing.

70 The play's account of a Cyprus still under Venetian authority is, however, an anachronism, perhaps as much a mark of wish fulfillment as ignorance at a moment when Ottoman power and the threat to Europe was obvious. Though in the play the Turkish fleet is destroyed in a storm, the Ottomans had captured all of Cyprus by 1571, and, though they suffered a major defeat at the Battle of Lepanto later that year, Cyprus was never recovered and remained in Ottoman control until 1878.

71 William Thomas, in his *History of Italy* (1549), ed. George B. Parks (Ithaca, NY: Cornell University Press, for the Folger Shakespeare Library, 1963), notes that the army in Venice is "served of strangers, both for general, for captains, and for all other men of war, because their law permitteth not any Venetian to be captain over an army by land, fearing, I think, Caesar's example" (p. 78).

72 On the complex history of the resettlement of the Jews in England in 1655, see Shapiro, *Shakespeare and the Jews,* 58–62; for the deportation order for "Negroes and blackamoors," see *Tudor Royal Proclamations: Volume Three: The Later Tudors (1588–1603),* eds. Paul L. Hughes and James F. Larkin (New Haven, CT and London: Yale University Press, 1969), 221. On the historical context of this deportation proclamation and an earlier one in 1599, see Bartels, *Speaking of the Moor,* 100–17.

73 [Pietro Martire d'Anghiera], *The History of Trauayle in the VVest and East Indies,* eds. Richard Eden and Richard Willes (London, 1577), sig. Yy4ᵛ.

5

Forgetting Hamlet

> Whatever his personal beliefs, [Shakespeare] is in the most important sense of the word a religious writer: not a proponent of any particular religion, but a writer who is aware, and makes his spectators aware, of the mystery of things.
>
> Stanley Wells

Religion is, of course, hardly a new topic in *Hamlet* criticism. Philip Edwards went so far as to say: "I personally cannot see a way forward in any discussion of *Hamlet* that does not take as its point of departure that it is a religious play."[1] That may be so. In no other play, with the possible exception of *Measure for Measure*, is there such a sustained engagement with religious issues and in which religious language is so prominent. Stephen Greenblatt's *Hamlet in Purgatory* is only one of the more recent and most eloquent expressions of a critical tradition that goes back to J. Dover Wilson and G. Wilson Knight and, in fact, well beyond.[2]

It is now a commonplace that the problem of *Hamlet*, the problem *for* Hamlet, is his uncertainty about the nature of the ghost, an issue that can be decided (or perhaps can't) by turning to religious debate in the sixteenth century on the question of salvation. Even the Prince knows that spirits are likely to be devils and that he must have "grounds/More relative than" (5.2.538–9) the words of an ontologically ambiguous apparition to justify killing the King. Where the twentieth century, following Freud's student, Ernest Jones, tended to see the tragedy mainly in psychological terms,[3] recently we have been more likely to see it in theological ones. An individual's Oedipus complex has been replaced by the culture's complex religious history as the motor of the play. Theology has replaced psychology as the favored tool to penetrate the heart of the mystery that is *Hamlet*.

But I wonder if the turn to religion has come a bit too quickly, not in the history of criticism but in the reading of the play. The Prince is someone who desperately wants to speak *to* the dead.[4] When he first hears about the apparition, he quickly decides "If it assume my noble father's person/I'll speak to it, though hell itself should gape/And bid me hold my peace" (1.2.242–4), although scholars consistently held that this was the one thing that must never be done. Lavater, for example, while admitting that spirits do "shewe themselues vnto men," insisted that one should "Enter into no communication with suche spirites, neither aske them what thou must giue, or what thou most doo, or what shal happen hereafter."[5]

But students often ignore their teachers and their textbooks. Horatio, at least a bit more prudently, was hoping mainly to listen: "If thou hast any sound or use of voice," he says to the Ghost, "Speak to me" (1.1.127–8).

> If there be any good thing to be done
> That may to thee do ease and grace to me,
> Speak to me.
> If thou art privy to thy country's fate,
> Which happily foreknowing may avoid,
> Oh Speak.
> Or if thou hast uphoarded in thy life
> Extorted treasure in the womb of earth—
> For which, they say, your spirits oft walk in death—
> Speak of it; stay and speak. (1.1.129–38)

Horatio, unsurprisingly, demonstrates the more inquisitive and subtle mind. I have always imagined that he was at least the more responsible student at Wittenberg, and that Hamlet regularly asked him for his lecture notes. An Oxford student today would recognize his interests as being more or less identical with the current course of study known as PPE, or Philosophy, Politics, and Economics. As Horatio seeks information from the ghost, he traces the course syllabus's descending trajectory from metaphysical speculation to political consideration to financial concern: what might be done to aid your salvation and my own, what might you know about the military threat from Norway, and, oh, by the way, if you happen to have any buried treasure you'd like to tell me about, then "Speak to me."

In fact, the trajectory is not evidence of an economic materialism inexplicably, or perhaps all too explicably, replacing the subject of salvation, but a register of the very language that surrounded this subject. "What shall it profite a man, though he should win the whole world, if he lose his owne soule?" familiarly asks Jesus in both the gospels of Matthew (16:26) and Mark (8:36). But the history of the Reformation, one might say, is the history of changing spiritual investment strategies, mostly involving the ideal market timing for maximizing the accumulation of what John Jewel, like so many theologians, referred to as "commodite and profit."[6]

A 1553 proclamation for the reform of English coinage predictably enough claims that it would work "to the great wealth, commoditie, and profit" of the monarch's "loving subjects,"[7] but the faithful knew that true commodity and profit accrued only to God's loving creatures and must be stored in Heaven (Matthew 6:20), although Protestants alone insisted that intercessory prayer could not affect the accounting. In the 1539 *Manual of Prayers*, the first of the reformers' prayer books, John Hilsey, then the Bishop of Rochester, noted the omission of most of the traditional intercessions for departed souls. "They are no more to be applied for the dead than for the quyck," he insisted. Of "the offyce of the funeral," he says, "it profytes not the soul."[8] "Profytes," of course, here means something like "provides spiritual advantage," but the word can too easily be heard otherwise, as Horatio's train of thought suggests, moving from what may both "ease" the ghost's condition and do "grace" to himself to the wide-eyed fantasy of hoarded "treasure." But what else would one make of Bishop Fisher's comment several years earlier, defending exactly the intercessions Bishop Hilsey had removed from the traditional rite: "our own profyte and our own wealth hangeth thereby"?[9]

Hamlet's reaction to the ghost is different from Horatio's. It would have to be. The sight of what seems to be his father overwhelms any theological speculation, provoking thoughts about relationships rather than religion, about connectedness rather than confession. Though he would speak to the Ghost, it is to re-establish attenuated psychological and social bonds rather than to perform some act of intercession, or even of intelligence gathering.

Ghosts make it easier to imagine what it means to speak with the dead, easier at least to imagine that there is someone listening to our side of the conversation. That may, indeed, be their real significance in human culture, what determines the fact that ghosts are among the very few things that may actually be timeless and universal. I suspect this is because one of the banal universals is that we are mortal. People die, and ghosts let us engage the question of what it means to be dead. We want ghosts; we need ghosts, less for what they may tell us than for what they allow us to say. They give *us* another chance to speak that which we were unable to say while we were too busy with our own lives to talk with the living: "I'm sorry"; "thank you"; "I love you"; "I will miss you"; even, and probably as often, "I am furious with you." But whatever one wants to say, what makes ghosts unnerving is that we inevitably feel their presence as an accusation of having failed them and having failed ourselves.

This may explain and motivate several small and usually over-looked oddities in the play. It is often remarked that everyone refers to the apparition as "it," certain that whatever *it* is, it is not old Hamlet, but an apparition that has usurped not only the time of night but also the dead King's "fair and warlike form" (1.1.46). The neuter pronoun seems appropriate, even necessary, for such a "thing" (1.1.20) whose nature is unclear or for a spirit (angelic or demonic) that, as Milton says, "can either sex assume or both" (*Paradise Lost*, 1.424); but a gender-specific pronoun would be appro-priate if one believed the spirit was the ghost of someone dead, appearing in the "form" it had while alive.

In 1.1, Horatio, Barnardo, and Marcellus do indeed consistently refer to the apparition as "it," but less often noticed is that in the next scene the pronoun usage is more unruly. Horatio tells Hamlet that on one occasion he had seen old King Hamlet, and then adds nervously, "I think I saw *him* yesternight" (1.2.188, emphasis mine and throughout). As he tells Hamlet the circumstances in which he encountered what he now more cautiously calls "[a] figure *like* your father" (1.2.199), he still uses the masculine pronoun—"Thrice *he* walked" by the soldiers, and they spoke "not to *him*." Hamlet, how-ever, responds to Horatio's simile, and similarly denies that this was in fact his father's ghost. "Did you not speak to *it*" (1.2.214), he asks, and Horatio replies, now echoing the neuter pronoun Hamlet has just used: "I did/But answer made *it* none."

Hamlet's first response to the report of the appearance of the apparition is, then, instinctively to assume that it is not his father's ghost, but quickly he shifts pronouns. "Then saw you not *his* face" (1.2.227), he says in response to the description of the account of its appearance in full armor. With no new information, the masculine pronoun registers how much he wants it to be his father's ghost, however soteriologically unlikely that might be. Two more times he uses the masculine pronoun, each referring to his father's aspect. "What looked *he*—frowningly?" he asks Horatio (1.2.229), the adverb perhaps revealing a son who fears he has failed to live up to either his father's example or ambitions for him; and then asking, "And fixed *his* eyes upon you?" (1.2.232), seemingly wanting himself to be thus acknowledged: "I wish I had been there" (1.2.234), he says.

Hamlet's obvious cathexis carries Horatio deferentially along with his diction. Again following Hamlet's lead, Horatio returns to the masculine pronoun for the Ghost ("*he* wore his beaver up"), before he switches back to the neutral form. "*It* would have much amazed you," Horatio says, perhaps referring to the whole event, but more likely to the apparition itself. Hamlet notes Horatio's pronominal shift, maybe hearing it as a subtle reminder of the theology he had studied: "Stayed *it* long?" (1.2.234–5). But the masculine pronouns have unconsciously spoken the emotional connection that Hamlet feels so intensely. Achingly, he still remembers his father: "His beard was grizzled, no?" (1.2.238). Even if the Prince again will affect poise, or perhaps in fact recover it, with his cool "Perchance 'twill walk again" (1.2.241), any skepticism he may have felt as the Ghost was being discussed has disappeared. "My father's spirit," he says as soon as he is alone, "in arms.... I doubt [i.e. I fear] some foul play" (1.2.253–4). He knows it is his father, who has recently died while Hamlet was away at university.

But earlier in the scene, well before Hamlet has ever heard about the appearance of the Ghost, he has already revealed how much he is haunted by his father's memory, how "green" (1.2.2) it is with him. For Horatio, the Ghost is "a mote...to trouble the mind's eye" (1.1.111), but it is "a mote" that has already troubled Hamlet too, though in much more personal terms. "My father, methinks I see my father," he admits to Horatio, who anxiously asks, "Where, my lord?" fearing that the Ghost, which he has seen, has again appeared. But Hamlet sees his father only "in [his] mind's eye" (1.2.183–4).

He misses him, remembers him, knowing that so much had remained unsaid when he went off to Wittenberg while his father attended to matters of state and took the occasional nap in the royal garden.

Both Horatio and Hamlet see old Hamlet in their "mind's eye," the only two times Shakespeare uses the phrase. This is the second set of small, often overlooked details, and, like the shifting pronoun usage, it also subtly marks how much the early scenes of the play refuse to settle down to theology. "The mind's eye" sounds familiar, a timeworn cliché, but it was new. The *OED* lists no example of the expression before this in Shakespeare, though in fact John Davies uses it in 1596, in *Orchestra*, where he speaks of "showing the world's great dance to your mind's eye" (sig. C7ʳ). In its most obvious sense, the phrase provides an explanation for the spectral appearance, deflecting the unnerving thought that it is some real, protoplasmic entity apprehensible by sense. More than just imagination, however, for Calvin and many reformers "the eye of the mind is faith itself."[10]

But that isn't what the phrase means here. Horatio's "mote...to trouble the mind's eye" conflates two distinct notions, one metaphor, one metonym: the mind's eye and the mote in the eye, the latter familiar from Luke and Matthew, "why beholdest thou the mote that is in thy brother's eye, but perceivest not the beam that is in thine own eye" (Luke 6:37; cf. Matthew 7:3). Why, that is, do you condemn even the smallest imperfections in someone else, not noticing that your own are worse—all part of the biblical injunction that it appropriates but ignores: to judge not, as you will be judged in turn. Horatio means only that the Ghost is a portent of the impending invasion, a "precurse of feared events," as he says (1.1.20), trying to normalize the terror of the supernatural by subordinating it to the mundane fear of war.

Hamlet, however, when he says that he sees his father in his mind's eye, isn't talking about the apparition at all—he doesn't even know about it yet. He is acknowledging the psychological hold his dead father still has on him, his father's tenacious presence in an interior space that, throughout the play, Hamlet jealously protects. He is certain that his "father's spirit" is there, though not in any spectral form.

Indeed when he actually does see the Ghost, he, like the others, assumes that it is not his father's ghost. "*It* beckons you to go away with it," says Horatio (1.4.58); "*It* waves you to a more removed ground," says Marcellus (1.4.61). "What if *it* tempt you toward the flood," nervously asks Horatio, and then "assume some other horrible form/Which might deprive your sovereignty of reason/And draw you into madness?" (1.4.69, 72–4). But Hamlet does not say anything here to Horatio about his father. "*It* will not speak," says Hamlet, "then I will follow *it*" (1.4.63). "*It* waves me forth again. I'll follow it" (1.4.68). "*It* waves me still" (1.4.79). No sign now of the masculine pronoun he earlier could not repress, or of his poignant efforts to visualize his father's face.

Once he sees the Ghost, it is different. Memories are one thing; ghosts are something else. But initially, Hamlet is only interested in remembering his father, not as a religious act or a social performance but merely because he is still unwilling to say goodbye, persevering in what Claudius chidingly calls his "obstinate condolement" (1.2.93). Claudius refuses Hamlet's request to return to Wittenberg, wanting the Prince to stay in Denmark, remaining "Here in the cheer and comfort of our eye" (1.2.116). He wants to keep an "eye" on him, we must say, anxious about how intensely Hamlet's father still lives in the "mind's eye" of his son. Claudius wants Hamlet to let his father go, wants him to "think of *us*/As of a father" (1.2.107–8)— but his use of what is sometimes called "the majestic plural" tells us that thinking cannot make this so.[11]

Hamlet's conspicuous grieving, however, should make Claudius nervous, though not on doctrinal grounds. The recently crowned King cannot wish anyone to think too precisely upon the event of his predecessor's death. Claudius would prefer old Hamlet to be quickly forgotten. Even as he praises Hamlet's "mourning duties" as evidence of what is "sweet and commendable" (1.2.87–8) in Hamlet's nature, Claudius tries to manipulate Hamlet into giving them up. It is, he tells his newly-acquired stepson, an "unmanly grief" (1.2.94), "[a]n understanding simple and unschooled" (1.2.97), "[t]o reason most absurd" (1.2.103); but worse, it is a form of impiety shrewdly defined in terms designed to affect the Wittenberg student. It is "[a] fault against the dead" (1.2.102) and the sign of "a will most incorrect to heaven" (1.2.95). It is both "impious" (1.2.94) and "obsequious" (1.2.92)—this last not in its modern sense as "unduly submissive," but in its older technical sense as "dutiful in performing obsequies" (*OED*), the very "obsequies" the priest will enlarge as far as possible in burying Ophelia (5.1.215).

The King would depict Hamlet's grief as somehow Catholic, ostentatiously opposed to the dignified Protestant forms of "moderate" sorrow, which were themselves ameliorations of an extreme Calvinist providentialism, which was uncomfortable with any form of mourning at all.[12] The wearing of mourning clothes was encouraged only to comfort and consolidate the community of the living. "If any man wear such apparel of purpose to provoke sorrow, he is not to be excused," wrote Archbishop Whitgift, but "if for order and civility, he is to be commended."[13] Certainly Hamlet's mournfulness exceeds what the reformers would allow, emotions far in excess of even what his "inky cloak" and "dejected haviour" can adequately convey: "I have that within which passes show,/These but the trappings and the suits of woe" (1.2.77, 81, 85–6).

Some reformers condemned what Hamlet calls the "customary suits of solemn black" (1.2.78).[14] Thomas Playfere, for example, asked, since "the death which is in Christ, is life,...what need we then weare blacke mourning clothes in sign of sorrow, seeing they [i.e. the saved] weare long white robes in token of triumph?"[15] But if many theologians did recognize the psychological and social usefulness of mourning, almost all divines condemned prolonged and pronounced grieving. "Though loue commands vs," insisted Playfere, "yet faith forbids vs to weepe for the dead" (sig. E5ᵛ). Bishop Jewel anticipated Claudius's rebuke to Hamlet, asking, "Why may not Christians mourn and continue in heaviness?" before answering his own question: "Because it is no new thing for a man to die; because he goes the way of all flesh."

But he also insists that it is no bad thing: "He goeth into his grave as into a bed; he foresaketh this life as if he lay down to sleep. He shall shake off his sleep, rouse himself, and rise again, though we know not how."[16] The inescapability of death and the promise of eternal life argue against excessive mourning, which shows an absence of faith, as Playfere said, in God's redemptive promise; but perhaps Jewel's recourse to the full mystery of this promise— "although we know not how"—points to the uncertainties of the afterlife. Neither Catholics nor Protestants were very sure about how resurrection worked (Thomas Browne recognized it as a

"Mystery," but was proud to admit that, although certain Eve was created from Adam's rib, he would "raise no question who shall arise with that Rib at the Resurrection"[17]), but both Catholics and Protestants were confident that death was merely a "sleep" from which in some bodily form we would at last awaken. What they disagreed about was what happened to the soul after death.

But that's not Hamlet's concern, at least initially. Hamlet's grief is merely grief—not evidence of religious commitments, however doctrinally imagined, but of emotional ones. It is his father he misses not the Sarum rite. This is not to say that religion is unimportant in the play. Unquestionably it is, but religion comes after. Stephen Greenblatt has brilliantly and movingly discussed the post-Reformation world of *Hamlet*, showing how religion helps perform "the work of mourning."[18] At least the traditional religion does, which keeps the living involved with the dead through Catholicism's intercessory acts of remembering. But Hamlet begins just remembering. He is missing his father, not trying to shorten his penitential sentence. There are no sacramental hopes or soteriological controversies on display. Hamlet, unlike Horatio, is not wishing to do "ease" to his father's spirit or "grace" to himself, if only because, in what might be thought his thoughtless Protestantism (*pace* Claudius), he may assume his father's spirit is beyond help and his own must be unaffected by such remembering. As Bishop Hilsey said, "it profits not the soul."

Only when the Ghost appears to his literal eye does religion start to become the central issue, not when it exists in his "mind's eye." "Look, my lord, it comes" (1.4.38), says Horatio, and when Hamlet looks, when he actually sees the Ghost, only then does religion come fully into play, because now he must decide what *it* is. What was in his mind's eye was the memory of his father. Now what he sees could be an angel or devil or, however improbably, even his father's spirit. No wonder he asks of the spirit that has seemingly returned from the dead: "Say why is this? Wherefore? What should we do?" (1.4.57). Now what is at stake is Hamlet's soul and an entire worldview.

Protestantism, we know, has no place for purgatorial ghosts. At death the soul is transported to its final resting place. Recall, for example, Archbishop Sandys's exuberant claim: "the gospel has chased away walking spirits."[19] The spirits of the dead do not return, and ghosts claiming otherwise are always a cheat. The anti-Catholic controversialist John Gee, in his *New Shreds of an Old Snare* (London, 1624), saw the Catholic emphasis upon the existence of ghosts as merely an effort to encourage the unsophisticated to pay for indulgences and intercessions, noting that "Representations and Apparitions from the dead may be seene farre cheaper at other Play-houses. As for example, *the ghost in Hamblet, Don Andreas Ghost in Heironomo*" (sig. D3ᵛ). The Ghost "*in Hamblet*," however, claims that he is indeed just such a walking spirit as Protestantism insists he cannot be: a purgatorial ghost, "[d]oomed for a certain term to walk the night/ And for the day confined to fast in fires/Till the foul crimes done in my days of nature are burnt and purged away" (1.5.11–13).

Unsurprisingly the Ghost's expressed Catholicism has been read by some as Shakespeare's acknowledgment of his own father's faith, if not of his own, recognized and confirmed in the commitment Hamlet makes on stage to "remember": "Remember thee?/Ay, thou poor ghost, whiles memory holds a seat/In this distracted globe" (1.5.95–7).[20] Whether or not this is Shakespeare's own act of remembrance enacted in his Globe, the unmistakable suggestion of a purgatorial ghost, "sent to [his] account/With all [his] imperfections on [his] head" in the absence of those sacraments whose efficacy he asserts (1.5.78–9), certainly reveals the resilience of the traditional faith.[21] Article twenty-two of the *Thirty-Nine Articles* had insisted that Purgatory was "a fond thing vainly invented, and grounded upon no warranty of scripture," but the play's evocation of a purgatorial spirit literalizes Diarmaid MacCulloch's claim that the Elizabethan settlement was haunted by a "ghost…of an older world of Catholic authority and devotional practice."[22] And in that older world the charge to remember was not just the hope that the dead would live lovingly in the memories of the living but also the means by which the dead would come to live in bliss, at least partially by being remembered in prayers, which were believed to have some efficacy in delivering the souls of the dead from the torments of purgatory.

But if the reformers were often willing to recognize, as did the confessionally complex John Donne, "the generall disposition in the nature of every man, to wish well to the dead,"[23] they denied, as a

Homily insisted, that "the souls of the dead are anything at all holpen by our prayers," since "the soul of man, passing out of the body, goeth straightways either to heaven or else to hell, whereof the one needeth no prayer, and the other is without redemption." No purgatory; no intercessory remembering. "Where is then the thyrde place, which they cal purgatorie?" the homilest skeptically asked; "Or where shall our prayers helpe and profite the dead?"[24]

In a pamphlet published in 1590, Tarleton's *Newes out of Purgatorie*, the narrator falls asleep under a tree and dreams that "the very ghost of Richard Tarleton," the great comic actor, has come to visit him. "In nomine Jesu; avoid Sathan," the narrator instantly responds, "for Ghost thou art none, but a very divil, for the soules of them which are departed (if the sacred principles of theologie bee true) neuer returne to the world againe till the generall resurrection: for either are they placst in heauen from whence they come not to or else they are in hell."[25] This is indeed in accord with Protestant teachings of "the sacred principles of theologie," and also what Hamlet more or less assumes when he first speaks with the ghost that appears to him. But Tarleton's ghost is no less unsettling of orthodoxies than old Hamlet's:

> Why you horeson dunce, think you to set *Dick Tarleton Non Plus* with your aphorisms?.... What, do you make heauen and hell *Contraria immediata*, so contrarie, that there is no meane betwixt them, but that either a mans soul must in post hast goe presently to God, or else with a whirlewind and a vengeance go to the divell? yes, yes, my good brother there is *Quoddam Tertium* a third place that all out great grandmothers have talkt of, that *Dant* [i.e. Dante] hath so learnedly writ of, and that is Purgatorie. (sig. B2ʳ)

Rather than the pamphlet being a Catholic argument for the existence of purgatory, however, it is a Protestant satire disproving it, for when the narrator asks Tarleton to tell him what purgatory is and who resides there, Tarleton replies with a catalogue of the popes, all "except the first thirty after Christ" who went immediately to heaven "because Purgatorie was then but a-building," perhaps Tarleton's comic recognition of Protestantism's embrace of the primitive Church. But the rest of the popes are now "a-biding paines of Pur-gatorie... according to the measure of their sinnes": "some for false wresting the scriptures, others for ambition, some for couetousnesse, gluttonie, extortion, simonie, wrath, pride, envie, many for sloth and idlenesse, and some I can tell you haue come hither for wenching matters, thats counted in Rome but a veniall sinne" (sig. B3ʳ). Tarleton's *News out of Purgatorie,* then, comically brings the good news that purgatory is a Catholic fiction and that ghosts in reality do not return from the dead.

Protestants insisted that there was no scriptural warrant for purgatory: "the Scriptures acknowledge no Purgatorie but one, *the bloud of Jesus Christ purging vs from our sinnes,*" as William Barlow said.[26] Although Catholics often invoked 2 Maccabees 12:46, Protestants rejected the authority of the Apocrypha, insisting on *veritas hebraica.* The canonical evidence of 1 Samuel 28, however, was problematic. There a witch summons the spirit of the prophet Samuel to tell Saul what will happen in the impending war against the Philistines. This is the only place in the Bible where the spirit of a dead soul appears, and as such was the source of much commentary. In 1599, Thomas Bilson wrote that the episode "hath mooued much question in the church of God, whether it were *Samuel* in deede that rose and spake, or whether it were the diuell transforming himselfe into the likeness of Samuel, to driue Saul into despaire."[27]

Catholics tended to believe the former explanation, Protestants the latter. In the Catholic Doaui Bible there is, in the annotations on the chapter, a long note saying that "it is not defined nor certaine, whether the soule of Samuel appeared or an euile spirit took his shape and spoke to Saul," but the annotator holds that it is "More probable that his verie soule appeared, not compelled by the euil spirite but obeying God's secret ordinance" (sig. Gggg4ʳ). On the other hand, in both the Protestant Geneva and Bishops' Bibles opposite verse fourteen—"And Saul perceived that it was Samuel"—there is a marginal note: "to his imagination, albeit it was Satan indeed." The apparition was only *called* Samuel, wrote the Protestant minister Henry Smith, "As the books of Caluine are called Caluine.…[and] as he who playeth the King vpon a stage is called a King."[28] The Puritan William Perkins saw the entire episode as a warning "not easily to giue credit to any such apparitions. For so they seem neuer so true and euident, yet such is the power and skill of the deuill, that he can quite deceiue us, as he did *Saul* in this place."[29]

Like the appearance of the spirit of Samuel to Saul, a ghost that can actually be seen demands such questions. A father living in the "mind's eye" is merely evidence of poignant loss and of the reluctance to accept it. When Hamlet sees the Ghost, he must decide what it is that stands before him, if only for his own soul's sake. Immediately he articulates the options of his Lutheran training, granting that the apparition must be either "a spirit of health" (that is, an angelic presence bringing "airs from heaven") or a "goblin damned" (a demon bringing "blast from hell"), before deciding to "*call*" it "Hamlet,/King, father, royal Dane" (1.4.44–5). "Call," however, may be used here less as a conscious rejection of the options of a Protestant soteriology, as most commentators have assumed, than merely in the pragmatic sense with which Henry Smith notes that the apparition that appeared to Saul was "called" Samuel. But soon, of course, Hamlet's scrupulously Protestant options are joined by one more, as the Ghost identifies himself as precisely what at Wittenberg Hamlet would have learned was an impossibility: "I am thy father's spirit" (1.5.10).

Once Hamlet sees the Ghost, questions of religion then do become fundamental to the play, not just part of the requisite particularity of the play world. Once Hamlet sees the Ghost, he—and we—must listen to the unnerving words of the dead, instead of talking to him or hearing mainly what we want him to say. "[L]end thy serious hearing/To what I shall unfold" (1.5.5–6), the Ghost commands, although as soon as Hamlet commits himself to listening, the Ghost pulls the rug from under the exchange: "But that I am forbid/To tell the secrets of my prison-house/I could a tale unfold whose lightest word/Would harrow up thy soul ..." (1.5.13–16).

Listen "to what I *shall* unfold" and, eight lines later, "I *could* a tale unfold"—except for the fact that I am "forbid" to tell it. It is a classic give-and-take maneuver; building up the desire for what the speech won't deliver. The Ghost can tell Hamlet, and does, about his murder and his present detention in Purgatory. But the promised tale that would "harrow up thy soul, freeze thy young blood,/ Make thy two eyes like stars start from their spheres,/Thy knotted and combined locks to part/And each particular hair to stand on end/Like quills of the fearful porpentine" (1.5.16–20), that tale whose incredible narrative power the Ghost spends five entire lines establishing, turns out to be a tale he will not tell.[30] "But this eternal blazon may not be/To ears of flesh and blood" (1.5.21–2). The anticlimax cannot help but be heard as what is, at the very least, *narrative* bad faith.

But what is it that the Ghost cannot say? He has already told Hamlet about his sentence "for a certain term to walk the night" and by day his confinement "in fires," where his crimes "Are burnt and purged away," so all that can be missing is the harrowing detail of the pain, which would be incommunicable and incomprehensible in any case. That's the very nature of pain. It is beyond language and destructive of it.[31] But accounts of "souls in torment" relating their agonies commonly appeared in collections of medieval *miracula*, both to encourage sufferages from the living and to serve as warnings to the faithful to confess and do penance.[32]

In *Hamlet*, it is a narrative bait and switch: "Lend thy serious hearing/To what I shall unfold," the Ghost commands; but when Hamlet does lend him his ears (and the *Julius Caesar* allusion is not gratuitous: remember Brutus's response to Caesar's ghost: "Art thou some god, some angel, or some devil/That makes my blood cold and my hair to stare," 4.3.277–8), the Ghost offers something all together different than what was first on offer: "List, Hamlet, list, O, list./If thou didst ever thy dear father love…Revenge his most foul and most unnatural murder" (1.5.22–3, 25). Instead of a gothic tale of supernatural horror capable of producing some extraordinary somatic reaction, Hamlet gets only emotional manipulation ("If thou didst ever thy dear father love…"). Ironically, then, it may be less the theological credibility of the purgatorial experience that ties Hamlet to the Ghost than the psychological credibility of the bad parenting. Significantly, at least in the Folio text, this is the first time that the Ghost addresses the Prince by their shared name, while, no less consequentially, in Q2 the Ghost withholds it for a dozen lines until Hamlet has vowed to "sweep to [his] revenge."

The Ghost binds the Prince to him, committing Hamlet not just to "remember" but also "to revenge," as we have always known.[33] "Speak, I am bound to hear," says Hamlet, and the Ghost replies: "So art thou to revenge when thou shalt hear" (1.5.6–7). Hamlet is "bound to hear" and bound "to revenge" (1.5.6.7), "a man," thus, in Claudius's words, "to double business bound" (3.3.41). And Hamlet finds himself caught in the double bind, as he pledges (what can only be called) his faith: "Thy commandment all alone shall live/ Within the book and volume of my brain" (1.5.102–3).

Hamlet commits himself to a commandment—the commandment to remember that *is* a commandment to revenge—that other commandments, now willfully forgotten, would contest. "Remember thee?" Hamlet incredulously asks, as if his remembering could be at all in doubt, and he then confirms his commitment to remember by instantly promising to forget:

> Yea, from the table of my memory
> I'll wipe away all trivial fond records,
> All saws of books, all forms, all pressures past
> That youth and observation copied there.
>
> (1.5.95–100)

The extreme commitment to forget serves as proof of his commitment to remember. The pages of the "table," that is, the erasable tablet[34] metaphorically serving to record what he has learned, are now wiped clean, as he willingly—no, eagerly—forgets everything he has previously learned (especially what he might have learned at Wittenberg about both ghosts and commandments) in order to commit himself to his father and his father's cause.

His commitment is confirmed as he promises to "sweep to [his] revenge," a promise of which the Ghost approves but which doesn't earn Hamlet much in the way of thanks or congratulations. "I find thee apt," the Ghost says, "And duller shouldst thou be than the fat weed/That roots itself in ease on Lethe wharf/Wouldst thou not stir in this. Now, Hamlet, hear" (1.5.31–4). The Ghost's praise is immediately undercut by the assertion that Hamlet could hardly have done otherwise, perhaps another indication of old Hamlet's parenting style, but the classical image is part of the Ghost's instruction to Hamlet to remember, to avoid the effects of the oblivion-inducing river.[35] Now the Ghost can assume the radical identification of son with father that their undifferentiated name suggests, certain that Hamlet will listen (rather than speak, as he initially wanted to).

But to be Hamlet, to deserve the name, at least as far as the Ghost is concerned, is to be a revenger. The Ghost would turn Shakespeare's tragedy into the old play that Thomas Lodge remembered with a "ghost which cried so miserally [*sic*] at ye Theator, like an oisterwife, *Hamlet, revenge.*"[36] Yet what differentiates Shakespeare's *Hamlet* from the so- called *Ur-Hamlet*, as well as what differentiates the Prince from the Ghost, is that Shakespeare's Prince, if he can try to remember, can never fully credit the impulse to revenge. He is never quite as "apt" a revenger—the hard drive of his memory is never wiped as clean or is ever as exclusively dedicated to the Ghost's commandments—as either he or the Ghost would like, puzzling both of them, as well as generations of critics, with his inability to act.

Only when Hamlet can persuade himself that revenge is a mode of restoration rather than reprisal can he move toward its fulfillment, but that thought is exactly what he cannot sustain. He is disgusted by his own inability to act upon what he has been told: "this is most brave,/That I, the son of a dear father murdered,/ Prompted to my revenge by heaven and hell,/Must, like a whore, unpack my heart with words" (2.2.517–20). A mere twenty lines earlier, moved by the actor's passion, he was concerned that he could "say nothing" (2.2.499)—hardly a charge anyone else would ever bring against Hamlet, who speaks over 1400 lines, or 300 more than even the most defiantly vocal of Shakespeare's other characters—but now he reverses himself completely, deciding that to say anything is to say too much, is to allow speech to substitute for the revenge he has been charged to enact. No longer would he be like a player "in a fiction" (2.2.487); now he would be an actor in deed.[37]

Even this resolve, however, fails to motivate his action, for Hamlet's moral imagination has characteristically generated a disabling symmetry. Remembering is not enough, or maybe it is too much. Hamlet is "the son of a dear father murdered," and prompted by Heaven alone, he would be God's avenging minister. "Avenge not yourself," St Paul had warned the Romans: "for it is written, vengeance is mine; I will repay" (Romans 12:19). But in the next chapter Paul writes that the prince "is the minister of God to take vengeance on him that doeth evil" (13:4). As an agent of God's vengeance, Hamlet could act, and his vengeance might well have the authority and finality of God's judgment; but "prompted...by heaven *and* hell," revenge cannot sustain the moral differentiation that would make it justice. The copulative does not double the authorizing pressure; it cancels the essential difference between moral alternatives that is necessary to enable him to fulfill the Ghost's command.

The problem *is* the Ghost, which comes "in such a questionable shape" (1.4.43), which Horatio says "'tis but our fantasy" (1.1.22), which seems "a guilty thing" (1.2.147). Who or what is it? And the answer must be sought—can only be sought—within the field of religion. It is not like the ghosts that appear in *Richard III, Julius Caesar*, or *Macbeth*, ghosts that come to appall and judge the present, but whose own souls are not at issue. In *Richard III*, there is one moment of theological speculation, when Queen Elizabeth is mourning the deaths of her young children: "If yet your gentle souls fly in the air,/And be not fixed in doom perpetual,/Hover about me with your airy wings/And hear your mother's lamentation" (4.4.11–14). But if there is some soteriological doubt here, it is theologically unsophisticated and psychologically straightforward: it is only a bereaved mother's hope that before the souls of her "tender babes" reach their eternal resting place they may for a bit hover about her, like comforting butterflies, to listen to her sorrow. It is the state of her psyche that is at issue, not the state of their souls.

But in *Hamlet* this is exactly what is at stake, what is necessary to be known if Hamlet is to do more than merely repeat the past and blight the future by accepting the inevitable imitative structure of revenge. He needs to know what the Ghost is, understanding that "the spirit that I have seen/May be a devil…and perhaps/Out of my weakness and my melancholy…Abuses me to damn me" (3.1.533–8). But how is one to know the truth? It was easier when his father lived only in his mind's eye.

The play, then, isn't exactly what Stephen Greenblatt sees—that is, a story about how "a young man from Wittenberg, with a distinctly Protestant temperament, is haunted by a distinctly Catholic ghost."[38] It is true that the university at Wittenberg is a conspicuous anachronism in a play about a ninth-century Danish prince, having been founded only in 1502 by Frederick the Wise. It is a significant addition to the Hamlet story that Shakespeare seemingly found in Belleforest's *Histoires Tragique* (1559). In 1600, the year that *Hamlet* was probably begun, Samuel Lewkenor wrote about Wittenberg in an accurate if awkwardly named travelogue, *A Discourse not altogether unprofitable nor unpleasant for such as are desirous to know the situations and customes of forraine cities without trauelling to see them*. Lewkenor highlights the fact that "Duke Fredericke...erected in this citie an University, about the year 1502, which since in this latter age is growen famous, by reason of the controuersies and dispositions of religion, there handled by Martin Luther, and his adherents: the Doctors thereof ar at this day the greatest propugnators of the Confession of Ausberge and retaine in vse the meere Lutheran religion" (sig. E3ᵛ–E4ʳ). ("Meere," of course, here means "absolute," not "measly.") Luther had been appointed professor of theology at Wittenberg in 1508, and by 1600, as Lewkenor makes clear, the reputation of the university, and the city itself, was tied to his teachings. The Augsburg Confession, mainly written by Melanchthon and agreed to in 1530, though in fact a compromise and reconciliatory document between the German churches, was widely seen, as by Lewkenor, as the statement of the normative principles of "the meere Lutheran religion."[39] What Luther actually believed became a matter of debate in Germany, but from as far away as England, what the university in Wittenberg taught and sanctioned was confidently identified as Lutheran.

And it is of course true that the Ghost's account of his death— "Cut off even in the blossom of my sin/Unhouseled, disappointed, unaneled,/No reckoning made, but sent to my account/With all my imperfections on my head" (1.5.76–9)—invokes a specifically Catholic sacramental world, in which he has been denied confession, communion, and extreme unction, and is condemned, therefore, to "fast in fires/Till the foul crimes done in my days of nature/Are burnt and purged away" (1.5.11–13). But the play neither confirms Luther's teachings nor the Ghost's account—although it does not explicitly deny either—and neither Hamlet's temperament nor the Ghost's nature can be adequately determined or described confessionally as Greenblatt's elegant formulation would have it. But this should not merely be taken as evidence of the oft-noted theological complexity, even incoherence, of early modern religious belief and practice. It is no doubt right to point to the play's contradictory or at least ambiguous religious gestures, but the problem seems to rest somewhere deeper. The problem is not that religion demands belief; the problem is that Hamlet desires certainty—and the credal problem gives way to an epistemological crisis at the heart of the play and arguably in Protestantism itself.

Think of the play's most famous speech, the most famous speech in all of literature. "To be or not be? That is the question" (3.1.55). In Q1, the so-called "bad quarto," right before the soliloquy, the King comments upon Hamlet's approach: "see where hee comes poring vppon a booke" (1603, sig. D4ᵛ). It is similar to the Q2 and Folio line "But look where sadly the poor wretch comes reading" (2.2.165), though in these versions Hamlet with his book enters for his encounter with Polonius. I think, however, Q1 may well be right, at least about what Hamlet is doing.[40] "To be or not to be" is arguably not Hamlet's anguished meditation about whether his life is worth living, at least not at first. It seems more likely to be an academic set topic that he considers, though one to which he is obviously drawn.

Some edition, anyhow, should put the line inside quotation marks, marking it as what he is reading rather than what he is thinking. There were such books that posed debating propositions, designed to allow students to develop rhetorical and argumentative skills, like Estienne's *Defence of Contraries*, translated by Anthony Munday in 1593, which discusses propositions like "ignorance is better than knowledge" or "drunkenness is better than sobriety," as ways of showing how "contrarie thinges compared one with another do give the better evidence of their value and virtue" (sig. A4ᵛ). Certainly the audience of *Hamlet* when it was played at "the two Vniuersities of Cambridge and Oxford," as the title page of Q1 has it, would have recognized the *argumentum in ultramque partem*, and Ophelia, of course, does recall Hamlet, at least in part, as a scholar (3.1.150).

Hamlet at least begins like one: "To be or not to be?" *Esse aut non esse*. Okay, that's the question, and he takes the options one at a time, starting with *esse*: how might we be? Is it "nobler in the mind to suffer/The slings and arrows of outrageous fortune," or is it preferable "to take arms against a sea of troubles/And by opposing end them" (3.1.56–9)? Two modes of being. But the phrase "end them" seems instantly to short circuit his thinking on this topic and leads him immediately to the other side of the debate: to think about what it means "not to be." "To die; to sleep—/No more, and by a sleep to say we end/The heartache and the thousand natural shocks/That flesh is heir to: 'tis a consummation/Devoutly to be wished" (3.1.59–63).

I think it is only with "'tis a consummation/Devoutly to be wished" that the soliloquy shifts to the personal, that it escapes the academic abstraction with which the soliloquy begins and that marks so much of its world-weariness. Neither of the "to be" options ("to suffer…" or "to take arms against…") seems particularly appropriate to the situation in which Hamlet finds himself, and, in any case, both quickly reveal themselves as unappealing: the first too submissive; the second too butch. "Not to be" then seems the desirable alternative, especially in his present circumstances—"a consummation/Devoutly to be wished," spoken perhaps almost wistfully.

"Consummation" is an interesting word, hovering between two meanings: perfection and ending. On the cross, Christ's *consummatum est* (John 19:30) marks the end of his life: "he said, it is finished," in the Geneva translation, "and bowed his head and gave up the ghost." And yet the Gospels also promise that "all things shall be fulfilled to the son of man that are written by the prophets" (Luke 18:31). "Shall be fulfilled": *consummabuntur.* Jesus's life is consummated making possible a mystical union with his flesh, indeed a consummation devoutly to be wished. But the consummation Hamlet desires is merely the "end" of the "heartache and the thousand natural shocks that [our] flesh is heir to," and it is, therefore, the adverb rather than the noun that poses the difficulty.

Can one wish that consummation "devoutly"? It is fine if it merely means "ardently." But that isn't the usual use of the word; indeed the *OED* lists this occurrence in *Hamlet* as its earliest example of the word used in this sense, if indeed it is. Hamlet's disgust at the world may lead him *ardently* to wish this consummation, but he cannot wish it *devoutly*, in its usual sense of "religiously" or "piously," because, as he knows, "the Everlasting" has "fixed/His canon 'gainst self-slaughter" (1.2.131–2). (By the way, my favorite textual variant in *Hamlet* is the reading of this line in Q2: "oh that the euerlasting had not set his canon 'gainst seale-slaughter," turning the prohibition against suicide into an environmental commitment.)

Suicide is damnable, an offense against God born of despair.[41] Hamlet may not, as the gravedigger has it, "willfully [seek his] own salvation" (5.1.2). He may indeed hope that his "too too" solid, sallied, or sullied "flesh would melt, thaw, and resolve itself into a dew" (1.2.129–3). The line parallels St Paul's desire in Philippians "to be

dissolved and to be with Christ" (1:23), but, as Henry Smith said in
a sermon on the biblical text, we may not make ourselves "authors
of life and death," and he finds the prohibition in the sixth commandment: "If thou maist not kill another, much less maist thou kill
thy selfe."[42] And it is worth remembering that the sixth commandment was used also to condemn revenge.[43]

In committing himself to the Ghost—"thy commandment all
alone shall live within the book and volume of my brain"—Hamlet
claims to have broken free of the binding nature of the sixth commandment. But in the soliloquy the ambiguous adverb, "devoutly,"
must prompt an unnerving flicker of thought that such a consummation might not be so devoutly wished, and so Hamlet turns back
to the exercise, returning to the equation: "To die: to sleep."

It is, of course, a commonplace. We saw it earlier in Bishop
Jewel's promise that we go into our grave "as into a bed," entering
into a sleep that we shall "shake off" as we "rise again." Edward
Hutchins similarly promised that "death is but a sleepe, and a short
sleepe, out of the which we, and al our brethren, sisters, and friends
that are departed in the Lorde, shal rise more fresh than euer we
were."[44] And William Perkins too: "death in the old & new Testament is made but a sleepe, and the graue a bed...wherein a man
rest nothing at all troubled with dreames or fantasies."[45]

But for Hamlet the familiar metaphor, however conventional, is
hardly comforting. He gets as far as "to sleep," but then the theologians' reassurance, particularly Perkins's, fails him: "To sleep, perchance to dream—ay, there's the rub,/For in that sleep of death
what dreams may come/When we have shuffled off this mortal
coil/Must give us pause" (3.1.64–7). At least in the Folio text, he
had earlier admitted that he could have "counted" himself "a king
of infinite space" had he not had "bad dreams" (2.2.252–4, F only).
So if "that sleep of death" opens the possibility of bad dreams, perhaps it is not "not to be" at all, but only a more limited and less
desirable form of being. So much for the metaphor's reassurance.
"If it were but a sleepe," admits Henry Smith, "no man would feare
it at all."[46]

"To be or not be" in fact can *only* be an academic question. We
do not choose to be, and if we do reject the uncertain alternative,
which in some sense might be chosen, it is because we prefer to

"bear those ills we have/Than fly to others we know not of" (3.1.80–1). Claudio in *Measure for Measure* similarly decides that "The weariest and most loathed worldly life...is a paradise/To what we fear of death" (3.1.128–31).[47] The investigation of the "contraries" falters with the inscrutability of the metaphysical world. Hamlet cannot know what it means "not to be," since death is "The undiscovered country from whose bourn/No traveller returns" (3.1.78–9).

Right. Oh, except for the fact that Hamlet has spent the entire first half of the play thinking about and speaking with an apparition who he has decided is exactly such a traveler. It is an astonishing line.[48] Even if Hamlet means only to note the irreversibility of death, here it is an absolutely bizarre turn of phrase for a man whose almost every action has been driven by the possibility that the grave in which his father was buried "Hath oped his ponderous and marble jaws" and "cast" him "up again" (1.4.50–1).[49]

Remembering is indeed the crucial and contested action of the play, but it seems Hamlet has incredibly forgotten what should have been impossible to forget.[50] An unforgettable ghost that is, astonishingly, forgotten; a story that cries out to be remembered but that is forbidden to be told; the ghost's bad faith and perhaps the Prince's good instincts in repressing it; a father's emotional manipulations and a son's inability to forget these. "Remember me," the Ghost has commanded, but Hamlet's memory here seems incredibly short, though he too will urge remembrance. Within ten lines, Hamlet will address Ophelia as she enters, "Nymph, in thy orisons/Be all my sins remembered" (3.1.88–9), and three lines after that Ophelia will return to him the "remembrances" that she has "longed long to redeliver" (3.1.92–3). And when the Ghost reappears to Hamlet in Gertrude's chamber, it is, significantly, to remind him: "Do not forget!" (3.4.106), for apparently he has. Forgetting almost always seems easier. Even when Hamlet first sees Horatio, recently come to Elsinore from Wittenberg for the funeral, he greets him oddly: "Horatio?—or I do forget myself" (1.2.161).[51]

Earlier, of course, Claudius had upbraided him for the "stubbornness" (1.2.94) of his memory, his refusal to limit his sorrow for his father to some appropriate "term" (1.2.91), but the stubbornness of his memory was for his father. The astonishing act of forgetting is of the Ghost. Always for Hamlet there is some slight gap between the two, which he tries to close: between the memory, always "green," and the apparition, always ambiguous; between what is seen only in the "mind's eye" and what can actually be seen; between the father who has been killed and the Ghost that urges him to kill.

Should, then, Hamlet remember or must he forget? Our modernity is marked by a "redemptive myth of memory."[52] We usually believe that memory is virtuous: "those who cannot remember the past are condemned to repeat it,"[53] is the oft-*mis*remembered quotation of Santayana. (Those who forget the quote are condemned to paraphrase it, one might say.) But if we can remember, we usually believe, our lives will be better—better for us and better for those around us. This is the logic of psychic repair and the logic of our historical responsibility, the logic of psychotherapy and of Holocaust memorials. But it is hard to determine if or what Hamlet should remember or forget, hard to know if it is not perhaps those who *remember* the past who are condemned to repeat it.

Certainly the easier question to answer is *does* Hamlet remember or does he forget? Michael Witmore has recently written that in Act five, Hamlet finally manages "a cooperation with divine providence, which, paradoxically, allows him to fulfill the ghost's charge to revenge."[54] But perhaps in Act five it is less that Hamlet belatedly begins to cooperate with providence than that he becomes persuaded that providence cooperates with him. Remember when he tells Horatio about just happening to have with him his father's signet ring so he can seal the revised letter to have Rosencrantz and Guildenstern killed: "Why even in that was heaven ordinant" (5.2.48). What can one expect from someone who believes he was born to set right the disjointed time?

Yet, in any case, when finally he does kill the King, it is not revenge at all. He kills Claudius not to avenge his father's murder but his mother's and his own. Laertes tells him that the Queen has been poisoned and that Hamlet has been mortally wounded with the poisoned sword. "The King—the King's to blame," Laertes confesses, and Hamlet turns on Claudius in fury: "The point envenomed too? Then, venom, to thy work" (5.2.305–6), stabbing the King with the same sword that has wounded him and then forcing him to drink from the same cup that killed his mother: a double death for a double crime. Laertes dies thinking about his father as he tries to exchange "forgiveness" with Hamlet: "Mine and my father's death come not upon thee/Nor thine on me" (5.2.314–15). But Hamlet dies with not a single word about the father he has sworn to remember. The act he finally commits is reflex rather than revenge. "That's for remembrance" (4.5.169), he *might* have said, as he kills the King, but he doesn't; that, of course, is Ophelia's line.

Hamlet does forget. But, then again, perhaps he should. Revenge is less "a kind of wild justice," as Bacon thought, than a kind of psychopathic remembering, and maybe the "law ought to weed it out."[55] One needs to forget in order to break the imitative chain that inevitably turns the avenger into an image of the villain who demands the revenge in the first place, unable to originate an action but only able to react to and to re-enact the original crime. And Hamlet's notorious delay may be attributed as much to his resistance to accept his imitative relation either to the ghostly simulacrum of his father, who urges him to revenge, or to the smiling villain of an uncle, who would be its object, as to his uncertainty about who or what has prompted him to it in the first place. He ultimately is unable to act on the word of the Ghost, because he has no way of knowing what it is. He can *call* it "Hamlet, King, father, royal Dane," but it is always an ambiguous ghost, whose nature is not confirmed nor is it confirmable by any theology the play has to offer. Hamlet *is* able to act on the actions of his murderous stepfather, but not before he has become, like his father, one of Claudius's victims. For Freud "the work of remembering" is the way out of the "compulsion to repeat."[56] For Shakespeare, perhaps it lies in the possibility of forgetting.

Ultimately Hamlet neither remembers nor revenges, but he, exactly like the Ghost, "could a tale unfold," though he too refuses to unfold it while demanding to be remembered.[57] "Oh, I could tell you—/But let it be," says Hamlet, before instructing Horatio to "report me and my cause aright/to the unsatisfied" (5.2.321–4). "Absent thee from felicity awhile," he begs, "And in this harsh world draw thy breath in pain/To tell my story" (5.2.331–3). In his final speech, Hamlet gives Fortinbras his "dying voice" (5.2.340), that is, his vote or nomination to succeed to the Danish crown. But it is Horatio who actually has his dying voice, though in a different sense: "So tell him," Hamlet orders Horatio "with th'occurants more and less/Which have solicited. The rest is silence" (5.2.341–2). Hamlet dies characteristically punning. Does "rest" mean remainder or repose? Is it that he can say nothing else, or that silence will come now as a relief, the silence of the grave, the consummation he has however devoutly wished?

But if the pun, like the silence, exactly marks the ambiguity that the play insists upon, in either sense here it only cues *his* silence. Horatio will fill the void, speaking "from his mouth whose voice will draw no more" (5.2.376), although the story Horatio tells cannot be exactly what Hamlet had hoped for. Horatio's account is the story "Of carnal, bloody, and unnatural acts,/Of accidental judgments, casual slaughters,/Of deaths put on by cunning and for no cause,/And in this upshot, purposes mistook/Fallen on th' inventers' heads" (5.2.365–9). Hardly the story Hamlet imagines to redeem his "wounded name," and also not the story of Shakespeare's play, in which the problems of trying to respond and be responsible to the past are so much more complex and so much less contingent.

Not a word from Horatio, however, of purgatorial ghosts, burial rites, or theological controversies. Perhaps he too has forgotten. But then again there *are* a lot of bodies on the stage: Hamlet's, Laertes's, Claudius's, Gertrude's. Also, Ophelia has drowned, though whether she came to the water or the water came to her is in doubt, and her father has been stabbed to death and his body callously stuffed beneath the stairs. And Rosencrantz and Guildenstern have been sent to their deaths, like all the rest, with no "shriving time allowed" (5.247), the news of their fate reaching England just as Hamlet dies. The play, we often forget, distracted by all of its linguistic richness and metaphysical density, is a bloodbath. Maybe Horatio's promised story "of carnal, bloody, and unnatural acts" is not so far off the mark after all. These dispiriting ends all seem very much "rough hewn," with no obvious marks of any divinity having shaped them.

Horatio had tried to suggest at least one such shaping. "Now cracks a noble heart," he says as Hamlet dies: "Good night, sweet Prince,/And flights of angels sing thee to thy rest" (5.2.343–5). Horatio picks up Hamlet's final pun even as he echoes the Sarum burial rite: *In paradisum deducant te Angeli. . . . Chorus Anglorum te suscipiat, et cum Lazaro quondam paupere aeternam habeas requiem.*[58] (May angels lead you to paradise…may a choir of angels receive you, and with Lazarus, who was once poor, may you have eternal rest.) At Ophelia's burial, the priest, in his scrupulousness about the burial of suicides, refused "To sing a requiem and such rest to her/As to peace-parted souls" (5.1.226–7).

Horatio would promise an even more exalted requiem for a soul who may not have been much more "peace-parted" than Ophelia was. But if his hopes for his friend are indeed expressed in words "haunted…by the traditional Latin burial service," as Susan Brigden has said,[59] the new world of the play immediately asserts itself. Horatio's very next line is "why does the drum come hither?" Instead of the chorus of angels we hear the military march, announcing Fortinbras's arrival as he comes to claim his "rights of memory in this kingdom" (5.2.373), rights that cancel the effects of old Hamlet's victory over old Fortinbras and that allow at least one son a satisfying revenge. And though Fortinbras generously orders a service for Hamlet's death, it is a military funeral, with only "the soldiers' music and the rite of war" (5.2.383) to sing Hamlet to his rest, remembering him, or misremembering him, in the last of the play's consistently "maimed" ceremonies.[60]

Religion obviously matters in this play. It is intensely saturated with religious language, religious practices, and religious ideas, but their presence neither exhausts nor explains the play's mysteries, and they function neither as an index of Shakespeare's faith nor as a prompt or challenge to our own. And for all the play's emphatic post-Reformation vocabulary and concerns, it is worth noting as Margreta de Grazia has done, that Hamlet's last words are not about theological matters at all but about political ones.[61] Reformers like William Perkins had insisted that dying well usually involved "*Last words*, which for the most part in them that truly served God, are very excellent & comfortable and full of grace."[62] Hamlet's aren't. But *Hamlet* isn't some dramatic *ars moriendi*. It doesn't seem to know what dying well might mean. In fact, it isn't even sure what dying means. And in the space of those uncertainties the play transforms theology into tragedy.

Notes

1 Edwards, "Tragic Balance in *Hamlet*," *Shakespeare Survey* 36 (1983), 45.

2 Greenblatt, *Hamlet and Purgatory* (Princeton, NJ: Princeton University Press, 2001); G. Wilson Knight, *The Wheel of Fire: Interpretations of Shakespearean Tragedy* (Oxford: Oxford University Press, 1930), esp. 17–49. J. Dover Wilson, *What Happens in Hamlet?* (Cambridge: Macmillan, 1935); Robert H. West, *The Invisible World: A Study of Pneumatology in Elizabethan Drama* (Athens, GA: University of Georgia Press, 1939). It may well be Hermann Ulrici who first proposed a religious reading of the play: "the whole drama is expressly founded on the higher moral doctrines of *Christianity*." See his *Shakespeare's Dramatic Art* (1846), trans. L. Dora Schmitz (London: George Bell and Sons, 1876), vol. 1, 490. Among the many fine examples of more recent work on *Hamlet* and religion, see Arthur McGee, *The Elizabethan Hamlet* (New Haven, CT: Yale University Press, 1987); Anthony Low, "*Hamlet* and the Ghost of Purgatory: Intimations of Killing the Father," *ELR* 29 (1999), 443–67; Richard McCoy, "A Wedding and Four Funerals: Conjunction and Commemoration in *Hamlet*," *Shakespeare Survey* 54 (2001), 122–39; John E. Curran, Jr., "*Hamlet*," *Protestantism, and the Mourning of Contingency: Not To Be* (Aldershot: Ashgate, 2006); Kristen Poole, *Supernatural Environments in Shakespeare's England: Spaces of Demonism, Divinity, and Drama* (Cambridge: Cambridge University Press, 2011), 95–135; and Daniel Swift, *Shakespeare's Common Prayers: The Book of Common Prayer and the Elizabethan Age* (Oxford: Oxford University Press, 2013), esp. 140–60.

3 Ernest Jones, *Hamlet and Oedipus* (first published in 1910 in the *American Journal of Psychology*; in book form in 1949), but Freud had already discovered the relationship; see *The Interpretation of Dreams* (*Die Traumdeutung*,1900), trans. James Strachey (New York: Basic Books, 1955), 282–3. See also Jacques Lacan's "Desire and in the Interpretation of Desire in *Hamlet*," trans. James Hulbert, in *Literature and Psychoanalysis: the Question of Reading: Otherwise*, ed. Soshana Felman (Baltimore, MD: The Johns Hopkins University Press, 1982), 11–52; and Nicolas Abraham, "The Phantom of Hamlet or the Sixth Act preceded by the Intermission of the Truth," in *The Shell and the Kernel: Renewals of Psychoanalysis*, by Nicholas Abraham and Maria Torek, trans. Nicholas T. Rand (Chicago, IL: University of Chicago Press, 1994), 187–205. There are of course many fine psychoanalytically inspired studies of *Hamlet*; see, for example, Jacqueline Rose, "Hamlet—the 'Mona Lisa' of Literature," in *Sexuality in the Field of Vision* (London: Verso, 1986), 123–40; and Nouri Gana, "Remembering Forbidding Mourning: Repetition, Indifference, Melanxiety, Hamlet," *Mosaic* 37 (2004), 59–78.

4 See A. D. Nuttall's "*Hamlet:* Conversations with the Dead," in *British Academy Shakespeare Lectures 1980–89*, ed. E. A. J. Honigmann (Oxford: for the British Academy by Oxford University Press, 1993), 213–29. And, of course, Stephen Greenblatt motivates his critical engagement

with the past: "I began with the desire to speak with the dead," in *Shakespearean Negotiations: The Circulation of Social Energy in Renaissance England* (Berkeley and Los Angeles, CA: University of California Press, 1988), 1.

5 Ludwig Lavater (Lewes Lavaterus), *Of Ghosts and Spirites Walking by Night* (London, 1572), sig. I4ʳ, Bb2ᵛ.

6 "Sermon on the Nativitie," *Second Tome of Homilies* (London, 1571), sig. Z1ʳ.

7 *Proclamation for the New Seuerall Monies, and Coines* (London, 1553).

8 *Manuall of Prayers or the Prymer in Englysh & Laten*, (London, 1539), sig. †2ʳ.

9 Fisher, *Here after ensueth two fruytfull sermons* (London, 1532), sig. C3ʳ.

10 Jean Calvin, *A Harmonie vpon the Three Euangelists, Matthew, Mark and Luke*, trans. E. P. (London, 1584), sig. L3ᵛ.

11 So much of the emotional drama of *Hamlet* is played out in subtle shifts of pronouns. Hamlet is "our son" (1.2.117) to Claudius, but his plural first-person pronoun only articulates the conventional royal claims of the mutuality of ruler and nation rather than acknowledges the bond of husband and wife: with Gertrude, Hamlet is always "*your* son" (4.5.80; 2.2.55). Similarly, the tension between Hamlet and Gertrude is signaled in their contrasting use of the second-person pronoun: "I pray *thee* stay with us; go not to Wittenberg," says an affectionate Gertrude (whose "us," by the way, is exactly the familially inclusive usage Claudius avoids), but Hamlet pointedly refuses the intimacy of her "thee." "I shall in all my best obey *you*, madam" (1.2.119–20), he icily answers, before Claudius quickly brings the awkward exchange to an end, assuring all present of exactly what it is not: "Why 'tis a loving and a fair reply" (1.2.121). There are Hamlet's shifting pronouns in his address to the Ghost, revealing his growing certainty about its nature as he shifts from "I will speak to *thee*" when he first addresses the apparition (1.1.44) to "Do *you* not come *your* tardy son to chide" (3.4.107), shifting to the semantic form with which he would have addressed his father while alive. And of course there are those seemingly unconscious slides into the masculine third person as Hamlet first speaks about the Ghost, revealing how vitally his father lives on in his memory even before the Prince has ever seen him.

12 Peter Marshall, *Beliefs and the Dead in Reformation England* (Oxford: Oxford University Press, 2002), esp. 265–308; Ralph Houlbrooke, *Death, Religion, and the Family in England 1480–1750* (Oxford: Clarendon Press, 1998), esp. 220–54.

13 Whitgift, "Tract 21," *The Works of John Whitgift, D. D.*, ed. John Ayre (Cambridge: Cambridge University Press, 1853), vol. 3, 371.

14 Lutherans had a more intense culture of mourning. See Anna Linton's *Poetry and Parental Bereavement in Early Modern Lutheran Germany* (Oxford: Oxford University Press, 2007). In England, questions about mourning were contested and do not break down neatly along confessional lines. I am grateful to Bruce Gordon for discussing this topic with me.

15 Playfere, *A most Excellent and Heavenly Sermon: Vpon the 23. Chapter of the Gospell by Saint Luke* (London, 1595), sig. E5ʳ.

16 Jewell, "Exposition upon the Two Epistles of St Paul to the Thessalonians," *The Works of John Jewel, Bishop of Salisbury*, ed. John Ayre (Cambridge: Parker Society, 1848), vol. 2, 865–6.

17 Browne, *Religio Medici* (London, 1682), sig. E2ᵛ, E2ʳ. For the early history of this doubt, see Carolyn Walker Bynum, *The Resurrection of the Body in Western Christianity, 200–1336* (New York: Columbia University Press, 1995).

18 Greenblatt, *Hamlet in Purgatory*, 247; see also Daniel Swift, *Shakespeare's Common Prayers*, 140–60.

19 Sandys, *Sermons*, ed. John Ayre (Oxford: Parker Society, 1841), 60.

20 Richard Wilson, *Secret Shakespeare: Studies in Theatre, Religion and Resistance* (Manchester: Manchester University Press, 2004), 52.

21 See, among many accounts, John Freeman's cleverly titled and suggestive "This Side of Purgatory: Ghostly Fathers and the Recusant Legacy in *Hamlet*," in *Shakespeare and the Culture of Christianity in Early Modern England*, eds. Dennis Taylor and David Beauregard (New York: Fordham University Press, 2003), 222–59.

22 MacCulloch, *The Later Reformation in England, 1547–1603* (New York: St Martin's Press, 1990), 6.

23 *LXXX sermons preached by that learned and reverend divine, Iohn Donne, Dr* (London, 1640), sig. Xxx4ᵛ.

24 "The Thirde Parte of the Homilie on Prayer," in *The Seconde Tome of Homelyes* (London, 1563), sig. Ss1ᵛ.

25 *Tarltons Newes out of Purgatorie* (London, 1590), sig. B1ᵛ–B2ʳ. Punctuation has been modernized. On purgatory, in addition to Greenblatt's *Hamlet and Purgatory*, *passim*, see also Peter Marshall, "'The map of God's word': Geographies of the afterlife in Tudor and early Stuart England," in *The Place of the Dead: Death and Remembrance in Late Medieval and Early Modern Europe*, eds. Bruce Gordon and Peter Marshall (Cambridge: Cambridge University Press, 2000), 110–30; and Kristen Poole, *Supernatural Environments in Shakespeare's England*, esp. 95–135, both of which make the case compellingly that purgatory was still a "live" issue and had not been entirely successfully sequestered into some Catholic past for many, or possibly even most people in post-Reformation England.

26 Barlow, *The Defence of the Articles of the Protestant Religion* (London, 1601), sig. T2ʳ.

27 Bilson, *The Effect of Certaine Sermons Touching the Full Redemption of Mankind* (London, 1599), sig. Dd2ᵛ. As Bilson tries to make clear, even Protestants disagreed about whether it was Samuel who had appeared to Saul.

28 Smith, *The Sermons of Maister Henrie Smith* (London, 1593), sig. Mm3ᵛ.

29 Perkins, *A Discourse of the Damned Art of Witchcraft* (London, 1610), sig. H4ᵛ.

30 Though of course the play itself may be such a tale; see Jesse Lander's paper, "'Like Quills upon the Fretful Porcupine': *Hamlet*, Horripilation,

and Supernatural Soliciting," delivered at MLA in 2013 at a session on "Supernatural Shakespeare" and his forthcoming book on Shakespeare and the supernatural.

31 See Elaine Scarry, *The Problem of Pain: The Making and Unmaking of the World* (New York and Oxford: Oxford University Press, 1985).

32 See Jean-Claude Schmitt's *Ghosts in the Middle Ages: The Living and the Dead in Medieval Society*, trans. Teresa Lavender Fagan (Chicago, IL: University of Chicago Press, 1998), 75–92.

33 John Kerrigan insists that Hamlet never "promises to revenge, only to remember" in his "Heironomo, Hamlet and Remembrance," *Essays in Criticism* 31 (1981), 114, but this particular reading seems overly literal.

34 See Peter Stallybrass, Roger Chartier, J. Franklin Mowery, and Heather Wolfe, "Hamlet's Tables and the Technologies of Writing in Renaissance England," *Shakespeare Quarterly* 54 (2004), 379–414.

35 See Garrett A. Sullivan, *Memory and Forgetting in English Renaissance Drama: Shakespeare, Marlowe, Webster* (Cambridge: Cambridge University Press, 2005), 14 and *passim*.

36 Lodge, *Wit's Miserie* (London, 1596), sig. H4^v.

37 See my "'His Semblable is His Mirror': Hamlet and the Imitation of Revenge," *Shakespeare Studies* 19 (1987), 111–24. Some of the material in this section has been adapted from this essay.

38 Greenblatt, *Hamlet in Purgatory*, 240.

39 On the Augsburg Confession, see Euan Cameron, *The European Reformation* (2nd edn., Oxford: Oxford University Press, 2011), 349–51.

40 Q1's placement of the speech may also be correct; actors and directors have long commented on the fact that the content of the soliloquy seems to fit better earlier in the play, perhaps even before Hamlet has seen the ghost. As long ago as 1904, A. C. Bradley expressed surprise that psychically Hamlet "is here, in effect, precisely where he was at the time of his first soliloquy," and noted its placement earlier in Q1. See Bradley, *Shakespearean Tragedy* (London: Macmillan, 1904), 132, fn. 2.

41 In *Cymbeline*, Imogen momentarily contemplates suicide, but realizes that "Against self-slaughter/There is a prohibition so divine/That cravens my weak hand" (3.4.76–8), and the gloss in the Bishops' Bible on the suicide of Razis in 2 Maccabees 14:41 says that "this fact is not to be approued, for that it is contrary to God's commandment, thou shalt not kill."

42 Smith, "The Pilgrims Wish," in *The Sermons of Maister Henrie Smith Gathered into One Volume* (London, 1593), sig. Mm6^r; see also Heinrich Bullinger, *Fiftie Godlie and Learned Sermons*, trans. H. I. (London, 1577), sig. Rr4^r. Although Donne would admit "a perplexitie and flexibilitie in the doctrine" of suicide (*Biathanatos*, 1648, sig. C1^v), few if any other clergymen defended the practice, even if the example of Razi and Samson troubled them. For two remarkable accounts of the social understanding of suicide in early modern England, see Michael MacDonald and

Terence R. Murphy, *Sleepless Souls: Suicide in Early Modern England* (Oxford: Clarendon Press, 1990); and R. A. Houston, *Punishing the Dead: Suicide, Lordship, and Community in Britain, 1500–1830* (Oxford: Oxford University Press, 2010).

43 Thomas Gibson, for example, says "God forbiddeth all cruelty and priuate reuenge in the sixth commandement," in his *The Blessing of a Good King* (London, 1614), Ff8ʳ.

44 Hutchins, *Davids Sling Against Great Goliah* (London, 1593), sig. K1ʳ.

45 Perkins, *A Salve for a Sicke Man* (London, 1595), sig. B6ᵛ.

46 Smith, "The Pilgrims Wish," *The Sermons of Maister Henrie Smith*, sig, Ll7ᵛ.

47 C. S. Lewis long ago identified the cause of Hamlet's delay as "the fear of death; not to a physical fear of dying, but a fear of being dead. Any serious attention to the state of being dead, unless it is limited by some definite religious or antireligious doctrine, must, I suppose, paralyze the will by introducing infinite uncertainties and rendering all motives inadequate." See his "Hamlet: the Prince or the Poem?," which was the British Academy Shakespeare Lecture for 1942, reprinted in *Shakespeare's Tragedies: An Anthology of Modern Criticism*, ed. Laurence Lerner (Harmondsworth: Penguin, 1963), 72.

48 W. J. Lawrence says it is "sheer absurdity" to make Hamlet speak the line after he has spoken with the Ghost, and speculates that the speech was originally written to be delivered "where 'O that this too too solid flesh would melt' is now to be found," which would allow the reference to "the undiscovered country" to be "informed with rich dramatic irony" since soon Hamlet would be given evidence of a such a return. See his *Speeding Up Shakespeare: Studies of The Bygone Theatre and Drama* (London: Argonaut Press, 1937), 57, 59.

49 In Q1, the "undiscovered country" is a place "at whose sight/The happy smile, and the accursed damn'd," not an entirely coherent account, but certainly less surprising than Hamlet's completion of the thought in Q2 and F.

50 Among the many fine accounts of memory in *Hamlet*, see Richard Helgerson, "What Hamlet Remembers," *Shakespeare Studies* 10 (1977), 67–97; James Hammersmith, "Hamlet and the Myth of Memory," *ELH* 45 (1978), 597–605; John Kerrigan, "Heironomo, Hamlet and Remembrance," *Essays in Criticism* 31 (1981), 105–26; Robert N. Watson, "Giving Up the Ghost in a World of Decay: *Hamlet*, Revenge, and Denial," *Renaissance Drama* 21 (1990), 199–223; Michael Neill's chapter, "Accommodating the Dead: Hamlet and the Ends of Revenge," in his *Issues of Death: Mortality and Identity in English Renaissance Tragedy* (Oxford: Oxford University Press, 1997), 244–62; Alison Shell, *Shakespeare and Religion* (London: A and C Black, 2010), esp. 106–17; and, of course, Greenblatt's *Hamlet in Purgatory, passim*.

51 Bradley noted the oddity of this in his *Shakespearean Tragedy*, 404. Thanks to Lisa Freinkel for reminding me.

52 Adam Phillips, "The Forgetting Museum," *Index on Censorship* 2 (2005), 36.

53 George Santayana, *The Life of Reason* (New York: Scribner's, 1954), 82.

54 Witmore, *Culture of Accidents: Unexpected Knowledge in Early Modern England* (Stanford, CA: Stanford University Press, 2001), 109.

55 Bacon, "Of Revenge," *Francis Bacon: The Major Works*, ed. Brian Vickers (Oxford: Oxford University Press, 1996), 347.

56 Freud, "Remembering, Repeating, and Working-Through (Further Recommendations on the Technique of Psycho-Analysis II)" (1914), *The Standard Edition of the Complete Psychological Works of Sigmund Freud*, vol. 12, ed. and trans. James Strachey (London: Hogarth Press, 1968), 153.

57 See Richard C. McCoy, *Alterations of State: Sacred Kingship in the English Reformation* (New York: Columbia University Press, 2002), 74.

58 See Swift, 159–60, who notes that Horatio's blessing is "a jumbled translation" of "*In Paradisum*" from the Sarum rite.

59 Brigden, *New Worlds, Lost Worlds: The Rule of the Tudors, 1485–1603* (London: Penguin, 2000), 367.

60 See David Bevington, *Action is Eloquence: Shakespeare's Language of Gesture* (Cambridge: Harvard University Press, 1984), esp. 173–87. See also Greenblatt, *Hamlet and Purgatory*, who notes the "sense of shattered ritual" found throughout the play (p. 237); and McCoy, *Altered States*, 74.

61 de Grazia, "*Hamlet*" *without Hamlet* (Cambridge: Cambridge University Press, 2007), 79.

62 Perkins, *A Salve for a Sicke Man* (London, 1595), sig. F5ᵛ, though Perkins does admit that the final words of the dying give no necessary indication of their "estate before God" (sig. B1ʳ).

Index

Note: titles listed first under Shakespeare, followed by other subheads for Shakespeare.